Further Praise for *If You're in My Way, I'm Walking*

"Thom Workman has done us a great service in painstakingly reconstructing the sorry tale of the assault on working people during the period of neoliberal ascendancy in Canada. But he has done more than this; he has also provided a penetrating critique of the Canadian Left, both its failure to fully grasp the capitalist processes which underlie the neoliberal project or to marshal the social forces capable challenging it. The final chapter is an impassioned *cri de coeur* for a reinvigorated Left political culture inspired by the rebel passion of class struggle as against the buttoned-down caution of the current labour movement and stultifying lassitude of the mainstream Left. The next Left, Workman compellingly argues, must be rational, compassionate and internationalist in its outlook; capable of remembering the lessons of the past even as it continues to imagine possible worlds beyond capitalism."
 — *Colin Mooers, Professor and Director, Graduate Program in Communication and Culture, Ryerson University*

"Not everyone on the Left will agree with all of Thom Workman's ideas about rebuilding the left. That said, his insistence that we need, desperately so, to name the capitalist enemy clearly needs to be assimilated into the Left's every conscious thought and act. Class politics, as Workman insists, must be revived. The unions have to be remade into forces fighting capitalist retrenchment and restructuring. We need a revolutionary Left to make this happen and we do not have it now. *If You're in My Way, I'm Walking* should be mandatory reading for all of those who don't want the contemporary economic malaise to drive living standards further down, to erode basic human entitlements, to further weaken trade unions and the Left, and to extend the capacities of capital to accumulate more and more in the hands of those who live off the labour of the vast majority."
 — *Bryan D. Palmer, Canada Research Chair, Trent University*

"In this thoughtful and provocative book Thom Workman outlines, in unflinching terms, the profound failure of organized labour and the Left to mount an effective struggle against neoliberalism. He delineates how successive governments have eviscerated the social policies and programs that, even in the 1970s, failed to create a foundation for social and economic justice. Now, forty years into the neoliberal transformation, things are immeasurably worse. ... Workman challenges us to take on the daunting task of rebuilding the Left, a Left, he argues, that has lost its vision, its moral compass and its hope. This is a provocative argument, deliberately crafted to engage the politically aware reader and to stimulate heated debate. As such, it's a useful intervention that may well kick-start a debate on the left that is sadly overdue."

— Julie Guard, Coordinator, Labour Studies Program, University of Manitoba

"Workman's account of the events and policies framing the most recent economic and political crisis of neo-liberal capitalism marks an important contribution to producing a more complete understanding of the nature of capitalism and how Canadians have arrived at this point. If You're in My Way, I'm Walking offers a breadth and depth of inquiry that can only be produced by someone with a firm grasp of the complexity and dynamics of social change and the specific factors shaping contemporary political, economic and social events in Canada. It is all too common for people to draw parallels between the depression of the 1930s and today. Workman reminds us of some distinctions between then and now — the most important being that the Canadian left in the 1930s was in a position to offer real alternatives to capitalism. Today those alternatives are not well enough articulated or widely shared to constitute a just vision for the future. Workman's book contains important information and analysis for any Canadian interested in understanding current events, but I also suggest that it is essential reading for the Canadian left. In the final chapter Workman outlines elements that could be part of a strategy to restore and deepen left culture nationally and internationally. It is in this vision that we find hope."

—Darrel McLaughlin, President, Society for Socialist Studies

"If You're in My Way, I'm Walking is an important contribution to our understanding of the attack on the working class in the last half century in Canada. Readers will see how this attack has contributed to a worsening of the working conditions faced by workers. This book is a must read for anyone who suspects that capitalism was not, is not and will not be the solution for working people."

— Raymond Léger, Researcher, Canadian Union of Public Employees

If You're in My Way,
I'm Walking

If You're in My Way,
I'm Walking

The Assault on Working People since 1970

Thom Workman

Fernwood Publishing • Halifax & Winnipeg

Copyright © 2009 Thom Workman

Editing: Brenda Conroy
Cover art: Beverly Briden
Cover design: John van der Woude
Printed and bound in Canada by Hignell Book Printing
Printed on on FSC Certified paper

Published in Canada by Fernwood Publishing
32 Oceanvista Lane
Black Point, Nova Scotia, B0J 1B0
and #8–222 Osborne Street, Winnipeg, Manitoba, R3L 1Z3
www.fernwoodpublishing.ca

Fernwood Publishing Company Limited gratefully acknowledges the financial support
of the Government of Canada through the Book Publishing Industry Development
Program (BPIDP), the Canada Council for the Arts and the Nova Scotia
Department of Tourism and Culture for our publishing program.

Library and Archives Canada Cataloguing in Publication

Workman, Thom, 1959-
If you're in my way, I'm walking : the assault on working people since 1970
/ Thom Workman.

Includes bibliographical references and index.
ISBN 978-1-55266-326-4

1. Working class--Canada. 2. Right and left (Political science).
3. Neoliberalism--Canada. 4. Labor unions--Canada. 5. Labor
movement--Canada. I. Title.

HD8106.5.W69 2009   331.0971'09045   C2009-904098-0

Contents

To those Canadians toiling away for a non-living wage.

Preface

Ignorance compounded by arrogance may mark the spirit of political leadership in these troubled times, as evident in the title of this book, but as we survey our contemporary horizons the spectacle of crisis and decay impresses us most. The onset of the acute economic crisis in 2008 merely intensified old news. Things have only worsened of late by degree, and if the left fails to speak to capitalism itself, to its grave defects, to its irredeemable character, then all the additional suffering brought about by recent developments will truly be for naught.

The pageant of humanity in the age of capitalism has been an illimitable web of misery. If we let the apologists define the present, if we let them pretend that things like rising unemployment, deepening poverty, the destruction of workers' lives, feckless corporate corruption, bloated capital markets and so forth are associated with the "crisis" rather than with capitalism itself, then we will have done a terrible disservice to working people everywhere. This is a decisive moment in history, and the left must make the narrative of the present its own, particularly by framing it within what is also known to be true about the nature of capitalism. The crisis is about capitalism *qua* capitalism, not an accidental set of developments linked to the depraved irresponsibility of the financial sector — itself a child of the relative unprofitability of the "real" economy.

The remarkable thing about capitalism is its ability to contradict Aristotle's ancient insight into the nature of politics. At the outset of the *Politics* the peripatetic philosopher claimed that all politics "aims at some good." Nowadays, as is widely understood, the goal of politics is capital accumulation — and little more. Public policy is singularly shaped by the accumulation preferences of the corporate world. The aim of goodness has been replaced by salutary promises of goodness "in the future." Along the way there is scarcely a thing that politicians will not say or do to get better rates of return on each dollar of corporate investment, and the unconscionable harm that this conduct has created for people around the globe is also well known. What we tend to think of as "politics," especially progressive political resistance, merely trails in the wake of this awful truth.

All of this is worsened by the fact that decent rates of profit are hard to sustain over the long haul. Rates of corporate profitability, for example, started to the fall sharply in the late 1960s and early 1970s. With these declines came a redoubled assault by capital on the world's working class. The goal has been to drive down wages and restore rates of profit. This is where this book begins. It focuses on aspects of this assault on the working class in the Canadian setting. Over the last few decades we have witnessed changing conceptions of working life, a deregulation of labour laws, falling rates of unionization, a sharp drop in labour militancy, stagnating real wages, the sustained presence of a large pool of low-wage earners and the expansion of the number of workers lacking basic protections, and the gutting of much social policy.

The severity of the downturn that began late in 2008 prompted comparisons with the 1930s and engendered hope that a *new* "new deal" for working people might be imminent. But there is a difference between then and now that tends to go unnoticed: in the 1930s there was a vital, active left, and real alternatives to capitalism were on the table. In the present era the left is moribund. Organized labour as a political force has been crushed. In the "deal" that emerges in the next few years the voice of the working class will be largely absent. Only a revived left can really change things. And so our task is just beginning — again!

Along the way one's debt to colleagues, friends and family inevitably accumulates with the passing of time. Encouragement, intellectual support and enthusiasm during the dog-days of any writing venture mean more than all of the riches of Croesus. For this I am deeply grateful, but I fear that my gratitude will never match their endowment of beneficence. I wish to extend special thanks to Elizabeth Hamilton, data librarian at the University of New Brunswick, for her kind assistance as I navigated my way through the labyrinthine productions of Statistics Canada. Deborah Sloan, Administrative Secretary in the Department of Political Science at the University of New Brunswick, always managed to make daunting tasks a little easier. Beverley Rach and Brenda Conroy at Fernwood Publishing graced this project with a blend of professionalism and skill that was truly humbling. And Errol Sharpe's unwavering support every step of the way simply made this book possible. Lastly, and on a more personal note, I wish to thank the "three cool cats" and their feline matriarch for putting up with your old tom.

2

1

The Neoliberal Rollback
in Historical Perspective

The last few decades have been unkind to the Canadian garment industry and its workers. Consider the case of the Golden Brand garment facility in Montreal. The plant manufactured suits for Moores, the men's clothing business that has sponsored the popular "Coaches Corner" segment of *Hockey Night in Canada* for the Canadian Broadcasting Corporation. Its host, the flamboyant and outspoken Don Cherry, is known for his gaudy suits (manufactured at a unionized facility in Hamilton, Ontario). Bright pinks and yellows, polka dots and flashy ties are not uncommon on this widely watched segment. When the CBC canvassed Canadians to choose the most popular national figure, Cherry made it to the top ten. His Saturday night slots came to feature regular tributes to Canada's fallen soldiers in Afghanistan. The contrast between Cherry's garish garb and Moores' modest attire — "well made" and "well priced" for the "well dressed," according to the company's motto — is almost comical, an advertising coup underscoring that Moores' apparel is suitable for those less eccentric plebians who tune in to treat themselves to Cherry's larger-than-life harangues.

The Moores workers in Montreal had reasonable cause to be hopeful about the future. They were part of a strong company with a long and distinguished history. The Golden Brand facility was founded by Martin Prosserman in 1961 and immediately began importing and manufacturing men's suits. After nine growing years the company was unionized. In 1980, Prosserman and his sons established the Moores retail chain across Canada. In 1996, the Prosserman family sold the successful Moores chain to an American consortium. Within three years the Canadian retail outlet had flipped again to the U.S.-based Men's Wearhouse in Houston, Texas, led by its Horatio-Algeresque CEO George Zimmer. Despite the changes in ownership, the Montreal factory continued to supply suits to the successful Moores retail chain in Canada and to the Men's Wearhouse retail chain operating more than a thousand stores across North America.

The success and corporate philosophy of the Men's Wearhouse company undoubtedly added to the confidence of the Moores workers at the Golden Brand facility. On its website the Houston outfit boasted that "George Zimmer and Men's Wearhouse believe in giving back to the communities" it serves. It rhetorically philosophized that "after all, being a socially responsible company is just as important as providing excellent customer service." The company's philanthropic commitment to "families and communities" was emphatic and rested expressly on the belief that community strength can be found by healing North America's menfolk who had fallen on hard times. The clothing retailer posted that it "has teamed up with organizations that help men who have faced homelessness, addiction, and poverty, and conquered them. The men served by these organizations have committed to changing on the inside and we are committed to help them reflect that change on the outside."[1] It complemented these lofty sentiments with an explicit commitment to all of its workers — male and female — in the company's annual report of 2006: "When a workforce is treated with respect and encouragement, there's no limit to where they can take the company."[2] And something was certainly working at Men's Wearhouse. It claimed to be the largest provider of tuxedo rentals in North America. Its sales of almost $1.9 billion in 2006 amounted to a 45 percent increase in just four years. In the same year its Canadian sales rose by 11.3 percent to $259.3 million.

Within a few years of acquiring the Montreal facility, however, the competitive global realities of the apparel industry bore down on Men's Wearhouse. In 2005, and irrespective of its rosy financial news, the company tried to make substantial cuts to its workforce at the Golden Brand facility. The vast majority of the employees at Golden Brand were women. Over the next year, several hundred jobs were salvaged owing to the strong resistance from UNITE HERE, the union representing the workers. The union was created with the 2004 merger of UNITE (formerly the Union of Needletrades, Industrial and Textile Employees) and HERE (Hotel Employees and Restaurant Employees International Union). Both founding unions had rich histories dating back decades. The new union, which would split again in 2009, represented more than 450,000 workers worldwide in the apparel and textile sector and the recreational side of the service sector, including hotels, casinos and restaurants.

The success of UNITE HERE was short-lived. By the winter of 2008, Men's Wearhouse announced that it was closing its Montreal factory for good. Its workers were devastated, and the city of Montreal, already reeling from mounting manufacturing job losses in the aftermath of the free trade agreements, was dealt another blow. Shortly after the announcement, the *Montreal Gazette* ran a headline in its business section entitled "Eighth Time Unlucky for Couple," a reference to the fact that one woman and her husband were about to endure their eighth plant closure since the mid-1970s.[3] Others were equally disappointed. One forty-two-year-old single mother supporting four children expressed fear about the future. "What will I do," she asked, "to support my family without this job?" Another worker, a twenty-four-year veteran of the Golden Brand factory who had emigrated from Romania, dwelt on the irony of the crushing news: "We came here as immigrants looking to make a better living and we gave so much to this company — now look what's happening." Another mother of two children, who had put in two decades of service to the Golden Brand factory after emigrating from war-torn El Salvador, talked openly about her feelings: "It hurts to hear this news…. To be kicked out after giving twenty years to this company — it's very hard. Without good jobs like these, how will we take care of our children and give them the opportunities and education that we didn't have?"[4]

UNITE HERE immediately launched a campaign to fight the closure. It organized a letter-writing campaign and demonstrations in front of some Moores retail stores. Workers in Montreal carried a coffin to one protest to symbolize the loss of their jobs.[5] Some Golden Brand workers travelled to Houston to present a petition to the debonair Men's Wearhouse CEO Zimmer.[6] "Moores and Men's Warehouse are turning their backs on hundreds of workers…" voiced the co-director of UNITE HERE Canada. "By shutting down Golden Brand and throwing hundreds more Canadians out of work," he added, "this company is sending a strong signal to Canadian consumers about how little they respect them, as loyal workers or as loyal customers." The international president of UNITE HERE emphatically added to this complaint while drawing attention to the money-grubbing bottom line of the corporation: "We're sick and tired of seeing good manufacturing jobs, like the ones at Golden Brand, lost so that profitable companies like Moores and Men's Wearhouse can extract even higher profits by outsourcing the work."[7] In late June the company offered Montreal employees a $3.5 million severance package. Lina Aristeo of UNITE HERE in Quebec seemed pleased with the offer, which would reportedly put between $3,000 and $9,000 in the pockets of each laid-off worker: "We are very satisfied with this settlement…. It is historic, especially for workers in the apparel industry."[8] Although the severance package at Golden Brand is uncommon for plant closures in the garment industry, each laid-off worker would only be receiving roughly three months of income. Any protestations of victory would have to be balanced against the fact that more than 500 workers, more than 80 percent of whom were women, were now without jobs and that their families would be facing the prospect of running out of money fairly quickly.

The closure of the Moores facility in Montreal violates our common-sense understandings about corporate health and hard-working people. A healthy company, it seems, was shutting down a factory. A business that claimed to care about "communities" was throwing more than 500 people out of work. Loyal, hard-working individuals, many of whom were trying to build a better life in a new country, were getting turfed out onto the street.

In this small corner of Canadian industry, profits meant job cuts, a healthy company went hand in hand with an expansion in the ranks of the unemployed and decades of loyal service were being reciprocated with permanent layoff notices. What sense is to be made of this? This peculiar intermingling of the good with the bad, of positive reports about corporate health and a hard-working labour force alongside negative reports about plants closures and sudden unemployment is staggering and leads us to seek some kind of explanation.

Sadly, gut-wrenching tales like the one at Golden Brand are so commonplace that we might be inured to them. Perhaps the Moores layoffs are more striking owing to the links between Moores, Don Cherry's oft-expressed support for everyday, hard-working people and Canadian troop commitments in Afghanistan, but stories about corporate restructuring and mass layoffs abound. To explain why such harm befalls working people and to account especially for the odd mix of good economic news (such things as healthy corporate profits and decades of strong economic growth) and bad economic news (things like plant closings and falling wages) over the past several decades, this book focuses on the evolving political accords that have framed the relationship between capital and labour since World War II. These political accords can be conceived of as institutional agglomerations and public policy paradigms that both reflect and frame the collisions between labour and capital. It assumes, as American commentator William Greider wrote in his sweeping survey of the global economy, that the collision between capital and labour is a decisive factor in the unfolding world: "The fundamental struggle, then as now, is between capital and labour. That struggle is always about control of the workplace and how the returns of the enterprise shall be divided." This class struggle registers institutionally. The political accords between capital and labour matter, and we can make much sense of the experiences of working people when we pay due attention to those accords.

But this is certainly not all that there is to the story. The institutional expressions of the class struggle interact with capitalism's *tendencies*, especially fragile rates of profitability, large-scale unemployment and high levels of poverty. A second crucial assumption of this book is that these inexorable tendencies create crisis and instability. Capitalist society can never ever sidestep such problems. Thus, using the term "dialectic" rather lightly, there is a sense in which the tendencies of capitalism on the one side and the political accords between capital and labour on the other side are "dialectical." The political accords can never make capitalism's tendencies "go away," but they can greatly affect the way a society responds to such things as rapidly rising unemployment or falling rates of profit. And at the same time, these ever-pressing tendencies put immense pressure on the evolving character of the class accord between capital and labour. The interaction between the two guarantees that capitalist society is never at rest.

In recent decades, the press of capitalism's inherent tendencies has combined with Canada's evolving political and institutional framework to strike hard at the working class. When compared with the immediate post-war decades working people have lost considerable ground. The new arrangements were refashioned according to the preferences of the corporate world. Along the way, more and more working people have endured awful experiences similar to those of the laid-off Moores workers, watched their wages stagnate and sometimes lose ground to inflation, become terribly anxious about the future, been forced into rotten, low-paying jobs and lost all confidence in the country's social programs. The gains that the working class forged in the first half of the twentieth century have been continually rolled back since the 1970s. The broad outline of this rollback is the focus of this book. These trends will only worsen as the global economy passes through the current economic crisis, and the ground that working people have lost is unlikely to be made up any time soon. To grasp the full implications of this historic shift it is helpful to review the two institutional configurations of the capital-labour struggle that have dominated Canada's post-war era.

The Fordist Compromise and the Neoliberal Rollback

When Canada's post-war era is approached from the standpoint of the struggle between capital and working people, two distinct eras emerge: the Fordist compromise (congealing at the end of World War II and continuing to the 1970s) and the neoliberal rollback (from the early 1970s to present). From an analytical point of view, both eras feature prevailing production practices, policy conventions and cultural trends that shaped the world and bore down on working families in their day-to-day lives. In keeping with academic literature that theorizes periods of capitalist accumulation, each era may be referred to as a "regime of accumulation" or a "social structure of accumulation."[9] By such appellations the focus is on the array of dominant institutions that stabilize and promote the reproduction and development of capitalist society, especially by trying to secure an optimal accumulation environment for capital. The terms are employed as a conceptual shorthand that identify and emphasize connections between prevailing economic, policy and cultural trends in Canada at different points in time.[10] The guiding premise is that capitalism is an inherently contradictory society and has endogenous tendencies that lead to recurrent and ever-pressing crises. Both of these features exact an array of moderating institutions to prevent seriously disruptive social conflict.[11] These institutional constellations evolve very slowly over decades of class struggle. Once established, the prevailing institutional configurations can be regarded as habits as much as anything — a production ethos, a dominant public policy ethos and salient cultural orientations all borne of social struggle and rich with captivating and dynamic histories. The consolidation of these institutional conventions permits longer-term periods of accumulation and economic growth by keeping social conflict within parameters that safeguard overall accumulation and permit the reproduction of capitalist society.[12]

It helps to consider the Fordist compromise era and the neoliberal rollback era from the standpoint of capital, working people and the perennial struggle between them. Beginning with the vantage point of capital, each institutional constellation builds in the productive and policy preferences of the capitalist class insofar as that class can secure them. And its influence is formidable. Capital — always in a struggle with labour, seeking to survive in a competitive environment and forever striving to innovate and find new markets for its commodities — uses every available means to insure that its outlook becomes the dominant orientation of the age. As William Carrol outlines, this process of securing the corporate outlook is politically rich:

> Corporate power is not simply a matter of commanding the heights of industry and finance. The consent of subordinates cannot be taken for granted. Much of the work of manufacturing that consent can be delegated to various intellectuals — in media, public relations, academe, etc. — but the corporate elite must exercise active leadership. The ruling class may not rule, but business leadership does reach into civil society and the state, recruiting support for a worldview within which the interest of capital in profitable accumulation is universalized. To reach effectively, to be a leading cultural and political force, the corporate elite must achieve cohesiveness as a business community, with a shared perspective on what is to be done.[13]

Ideas conducive to the strategies of capital will tend to fly over time; ideas hostile to capital's preferences will tend to fall by the way or be shunted to the margins of public discourse. In the end, the prevailing productive and policy practices are responsive to the profit-making strategies of the leading conglomerates of the business world, with cultural practices typically following, especially in the age of the mass media. It is in these ways that it can be said that the corporate world plays the leading political role in shaping society's dominant social and culture orientations.

Working people enjoy no such influence. At best, their preferences and interests are built into the institutional constellation only in a fragmented sort of way. Worker-centred or worker-friendly ideas can never be said to shape the leading practices of the day. Everything from the social background of most politicians through to corporate control of the mass media works to insure that this relative lack of influence of working people holds true. To say the same thing in a different way, the inclinations and preferences of working people tend not to find their way into government reports, media accounts of the state of the world, university studies and research programs, think-tank publications or party platforms in a way that is sustained. We must always be careful not to overdraw the Gramscian notion that the orientations and interests of working people are absorbed into the hegemonic framework of society. It is true but not too true; usually just true enough to insure the reproduction of capitalist social relations, but never ever enough to permit working people to escape the feeling that things are more or less stacked against them. "Received wisdom" does not tend to pivot from the standpoint of the working class and its interests, quite the opposite.

We can also consider the array of institutions from the vantage point of the broader struggle between capital and working people. It must be stressed that a "social structure of accumulation" protects capitalist society as a whole — not individual capitalists and certainly not working people *per se*. It creates an overall environment where accumulation is optimized in accordance with the expressed calculations of capital and where the social relations of capitalist production are rolled over. There is a sense in which each institutional constellation can be seen as a register of the relative power of the countervailing class forces at different points in time. Once congealed, of course, this institutional configuration shapes the day-to-day class struggles across society. In particular, the predominant institutions contour the conflicts between employers and working people endemic to the workplace, and they establish the parameters within which capital and labour confront each other on matters relating to the labour process, wages, employment and general public policy. The past thus continues osmotically to secrete itself through the pores of the present; "dead struggle" shapes "living struggle" via the constellation of institutions that frame a capitalist society at any given time in history.

The Fordist Compromise

Capital must always "be able to live with" the institutional constellation that defines any era, but this is not the case for the labour movement and working people. It is well-known that the labour movement fought against the institutional arrangements of the late 1800s and early 1900s at every possible turn, and it was only after a decades-long battle, characterized by undulating periods of advance followed by periods of decline, that labour's pressure led to the entrenchment of the Fordist compact at the close of World War II. The institutions of the post-war era reflected a *compromise* between capital and labour. This compromise amounted to a series of tacit understandings about the manner in which productive life would be managed within the workplace and across society and included an understanding that the "radical" left alternative (communism) would be eschewed by the labour movement.

To grasp the rich nature of this compromise it is best to start with the basic analytical motto of Fordism: "mass production for mass consumption." The capacity to produce commodities in greater and greater quantities is an inevitable offshoot of the capitalist way of life, especially as competition forces each generation of capitalists to refine continually their productive forces. These technological refinements invariably mean that work on the factory floor is continually "dumbed down," that is, broken down into a series of much simpler tasks. In the late nineteenth and early twentieth centuries, technological refinements encroached directly upon the skilled artisans who often controlled the labour process in the early capitalist manufactories. The artisanal labourers rebelled against the inevitable expansion of the unskilled workforce. The tendency to simplify the labour process received a boost with the famous "time and motion" studies of Frederick Winslow Taylor. Taylorism, or "scientific management," sought to make the labour process as "efficient" as possible, irrespective of its effect on working people, all for the sake of greater productivity. The capitalist world in North America embraced Taylorism in the inter-war period, and this added ideological fuel to the continual degradation of working life. Refinements in assembly-line production, boosted by the electrification of industry and the simplification of the labour process, combined with the expansion of supply chains ("backward" and "forward" economic linkages, as they are sometimes called), the maturation of infrastructural support and the expansion of a pool of would-be capitalist workers, especially through immigration, meant that capitalist industry in Canada could "turn out" commodities in unimaginable numbers for the first time.[14]

This transformation within a few short decades was nothing short of remarkable. Prior to 1850 Canada was not a capitalist society, in the sense that enterprises inclined to hire labour were subordinated to the rhythms of non-capitalist production, especially agricultural production.[15] There were capitalist-like operations, but the development of an extensive labour market, capitalist industry and developed market relations had yet to "kick in" in the way they had in the United States several decades earlier. A number of specific economic quirks in Canada delayed the extension of capitalist social relations in Canada. Most agricultural produce was consumed on the farm and locally, and very little ever found its way into wider markets. The farm families were self-sufficient in that most of what was needed to survive was secured on the farm, and what could not be produced was supplied by town artisans and small-scale producers geared to meeting local needs. Some production even had an itinerant character, as artisans sometimes roamed from town to town, and much labour had a distinct social character, for example, work bees.

Bartering as a form of exchange was common — a clear indication of the absence of extensive market dynamics and the close proximity of producers and consumers. The focus of economic activity in Canada pre-1850 was the farm and the small town. Today's growing "100-mile movement" has nothing on Canada of the early nineteenth century, where almost all things were made and consumed in the town and its outlying farms.[16]

From the mid-point of the nineteenth century, the hallmarks of capitalism, that is, private industry and a paid workforce, quickly came to dominate the economic world. Three developments in the transition from a pre-capitalist economy to a full-blown capitalist one were especially noteworthy. First, a capitalist class, which owned the manufactories (characterized by varying levels of skilled, manual labour) and later the full-fledged factories (employing relatively unskilled workers), took shape rather quickly.[17] Second was the development of a supply of workers in need of regular wage labour to survive.[18] Last, there was the fairly rapid growth of a market-friendly infrastructure to facilitate the movement of raw materials and finished products. These three elements went together to contribute to the relatively quick transition of Canadian society to a capitalist one, characterized by private property, wage labour and reasonably extensive market relations.

By the early decades of the twentieth century, industry in Canada could turn out a wide variety of commodities in impressive numbers. The challenge that always confronts owners in capitalist society is the difficulty of matching this impressive capability to produce commodities with the capacity of society to absorb those goods. Over the course of the twentieth century, part of this challenge was solved by the increase in wages in the face of pressure by organized labour. As was famously illustrated in the case of Henry Ford's $5-a-day wage, the business elite sometimes grudgingly accepted that modest rises in wages would help working people consume more products. In the decades after World War II wages typically rose faster than the rate of inflation.

The second way the problem of overproduction was solved was through the Keynesian public policy framework. The elite bought into the economic theory of John Maynard Keynes. Against the *laissez-faire* temper of the age, Keynes published his *General Theory on Employment, Interest and Money* in 1936. Keynes advocated the use of fiscal and monetary levers to maintain the economic effects of high aggregate demand (the so-labelled "illusion of full employment"), believing that the maintenance of demand would mean that the supply of goods and services would follow. Keynes developed these arguments at a time when the Western capitalist economies were wrestling with the severe undulations of the inter-war era. The policy prescriptions coming out of the *General Theory* were widely heralded as the panacea for capitalism's troubles. Keynes's timing could not have been better, and it would be hard to overdraw the impact of his thought. As Canada and many Western states responded to working-class demands for meaningful welfare programs, education reforms, unemployment insurance schemes and so forth in the 1930s and 1940s, and at a time when many commentators were beginning to fear for the future of capitalism itself, Keynes's interventionist approach seemed to be the perfect way to thwart capitalism's cyclical tendencies and maintain aggregate demand for goods and services. The Keynesian model helped to justify the expansion of a new, more "socially responsible" state. Social reforms were coming anyway owing to working-class pressures, but Keynes's intellectual imprimatur helped soothe the anxieties of the ruling elite and would help in their own way to maintain society's capacity to consume goods and utilize services.

As depicted in Table 1.1 the Fordist arrangement featured the consolidation and expansion of "mass production for mass consumption." Central to the Fordist compromise was an understanding between capital and labour that the prerogative with respect to the organization of the labour process would remain, for the most part, with management and capital and that capitalist social relations would prevail. The first part of the compact meant that the erosion of workplace skills would continue without too much resistance from organized labour. The second part of the understanding meant that labour would purge its own ranks of any radical, anti-capitalist elements. The *quid pro quo* of this political understanding for organized labour was the full-blown legal recognition of unions and the gradual expansion of a regulatory regime for labour in the economy. The process of purging the ranks of organized labour was riven with acute conflict, particularly during the late 1940s and into the 1950s. The long gestation of social policy throughout the inter-war

Table 1.1 The Fordist Regime, from Post-World War II to the Early 1970s

Production Conventions	Prevailing Policy/ Political Framework	Salient Cultural Features
• Consolidation of "mass production" for "mass consumption" • Promotion of "Taylorism" in the workplace and continual "de-skilling" of labour • Prominence of multinational corporations with distinct branch plant operations	• Keynesian countercyclical state spending • Growth of direct state involvement in economy • Institutionalization of social assistance programs, UI, pension and other state transfers • Legal recognition of unions and universal labour codes	• Institutionalization of mass or "pop" culture (continual displacement of class culture) • Ideal of the heterosexual nuclear family with male "breadwinner" • Cultural expressions of the standard "working day" and the "classless society" • Fervent anti-communism

period, especially in the areas of unemployment relief and welfare policy, congealed with the entrenchment and expansion of the Keynesian welfare state. And mass culture, dominated by the themes of the classless society and the heterosexual family headed up by the male breadwinner, adapted itself effortlessly to the emerging Fordist compromise, abetted by the post-Edisonian growth of popular music at the turn of the century, radio in the late 1920s and the dawn of the television age in the early post-World War II period. The politically soporific effects of the "feelies" (as Huxley dubbed aspects of the emerging culture industry in *Brave New World*) added immensely to the *hubris* of early post-war life.

In the early post-World War II decades the Fordist compact proved to be fairly stable. This stability was helped along by smoother economic growth after the early 1940s, especially when contrasted with the ups and downs of previous decades. Labour built on its gains. The rhythms of legality congealed as contracts were rolled over and grievance procedures were consolidated. The number of unionized workers continued to grow both nominally and as a percentage of the total number of workers in the economy, especially as white-collar workers in the public sector overcame their reluctance to mingle with the commoners and organize. Wages continued to outpace the rate of inflation. The house of labour healed its decades-long split between skilled and unskilled workers, a process that culminated in the formation of the Canadian Labour Congress in 1956. Tucked in behind this unification of labour was the political marginalization of radical elements within the labour movement itself, especially the more radicalized vision that was often found in the pool of unskilled workers. The labour movement and its political wings more or less tamed themselves and became a *bona fide* partner in the capitalist social system. It would never gain a seat at the policy table in the manner of the tripartite policy compacts among capital, labour and state that could be found in some European countries, but it clearly became a trusted partner in the affairs of the economy.

Capital prospered as well. It grudgingly accepted the gains of labour, acknowledging that this acceptance helped to regularize production,[19] while also retaining authority over the labour process. It enjoyed strong profits. And the expanding Canadian state continued to mediate class relations without undermining the integrity of capitalism as a whole. It neutralized the more salient threats to capitalist social relations with such verve that its anti-communist posture seemed tame only when compared to the McCarthyist excesses south of the border. It continued to build an economic infrastructure conducive to overall accumulation. And its social programs expanded to unprecedented levels. Fordism was based on an underlying political consensus regarding the rules of the post-war order: that capital would retain most production prerogatives; that working people would retain the right to unionize and bargain collectively; and that the state would retain the authority to backstop this trade-off. All parties proceeded on the assumption that the basic social relations of production would without question be capitalist, that is, comprised of wage labour and the private ownership of industry. The post-war order, more than anything else, shunted radical solutions to capitalism's ills off to the political margins.

In more stylized terms the post-war boom saw rising fortunes for labour, strong profits for the business community, sustained economic growth and the expansion of the Keynesian welfare state. This is referred to as capitalism's "golden age." Rising real wages, rising consumption, increasing rates of unionization and the quickening of commodity innovation aimed at consumers all contributed to a sanguine outlook on the world. The Western, liberal democratic states appeared to beat the boom and bust cycles that had plagued capitalism throughout its history. The non-communist world, it was claimed, had entered a new age of prosperity and social harmony. North American society seemed capable of resolving its conflicts without social disruption and crisis. The bounty of the post-war world demonstrated conclusively to many commentators that the idea of intractable social conflict, especially intractable class conflict, was a myth. In keeping with this optimism, the world's conflicts seemed to be relegated to the "developing" world. The Horn of Africa, much of Western Africa, many areas of the Middle East and the Indo-Chinese peninsula became mired in protracted civil and inter-state wars, and the profound role of the West in these conflicts tended to be under-acknowledged. The *hubris* of the age spawned a rich set of catch-notions ranging from the Ontario-born John Kenneth Galbraith's conception of the "affluent society" through to Daniel Bell's claims about the "end of ideology."

Such effusiveness, however, concealed the basic contradiction at the centre of the Fordist compromise. To explore this contradiction it is good to stand back and reflect on the congruence between lofty political struggles on the one side and the basic character of capitalist social relations on the other side. The foundational political movements for equality, democracy and freedom run headlong into the stratifying and oppressive character of capitalism. Capitalism presupposes inequality, domination and unfreedom, especially when it comes to its oppressive labour market dynamics. Enlightened political struggles, especially those of recent centuries, have always posed a basic threat to capitalist society, especially by taking the edge off the dire circumstances that drive would-be workers into the capitalist workforce. And outside the labour market such lofty social ambitions run headlong into a society riven with inequality and hardship. The struggles for freedom and equality have an "out of place" or Procrustean feel — they really do not fit in with capitalist social relations. Any substantial achievement of equality, democracy or freedom would undermine capitalism by weakening the oppressive social relations that drive workers into the hands of their capitalist employers or that divides society so blatantly into "haves" and "have nots." In a truly free and equal world capitalist social relations would wither of necessity. To avoid this inevitable outcome radical social ideals have been made to fit in a truncated or mangled sort of way, largely to mollify the working class. Accordingly, the challenge for the elite has been to contain the effects of these politically revolutionary ideals so that capitalist social relations, relations that are premised on inequity, anxiety and fear, could be preserved. And they — the class of power and privilege — came to be rather good at containing the disruptive effects of modernity's progressive doctrines, especially over the last century. The extension of the democratic franchise, for example, proceeded in a most calculated fashion and was only broadened significantly after the propertied classes became reasonably well assured that they would not be expropriated on the occasion of the next general election. Political progress without social progress sums the last century up rather well — formal freedom and formal democracy without a whole lot of substance.

A more pointed contradiction springs to life whenever the labour movement presses to secure its goals. As the working class presses for things like the right to organize, strong labour laws, the minimum wage, better wages and working conditions, and unemployment relief, their struggle challenges the desperate social conditions that typically deliver workers into the hands of capital and cuts into the autonomy of capital as it responds to accumulation challenges. Put a bit differently, when the goals of the labour movement are entrenched and made commensurate with lofty ideas like "living with dignity" and "justice for workers" two noticeable things happen. First, workers become less desperate, less vulnerable and more secure, and this, in turn, means that capital finds it harder to manage and exploit its once-pliant workforce. Second, as the labour movement grows in confidence and workers become more militant, the entire economic system is stressed by increased economic disruptions and social conflict and rising real wages. This gathering tension becomes especially acute during economic downturns or, worse still from the standpoint of capital, as rates of profitability decline. Since established businesses always need to shed parts of its workforce, since capital on the whole needs to create the social conditions that will insure a constant supply of workers, since insecurity and poverty always help to insure labour compliance, and since corporate strategists must be forever responding to the exigencies of accumulation, an energized, active labour movement fighting for its "rights" tends to be perceived as a potential threat to the entire system, not just an irritant for one company or one economic sector. The gains of labour are not merely a loss for capital; it is not a zero sum game. It is rather the case that a "new deal" or a "progressive social agenda" interferes with the oppressive systemic calculus and can come to threaten capitalist social relations at their core.

The carefully choreographed and highly restrictive development of social policy in Canada revealed this tension. The Fordist compromise ratified social and labour-market policies that were never terribly generous for the working class owing to the rudimentary need to infuse capitalist social relations with anxiety and fear. To prevent the labour market from either drying up (a likely outcome if working people felt that there were real alternatives to paid labour) or exploding (a likely outcome if growing confidence of working people led to rising militancy and runaway wage demands) clear limits had to be placed on developing social policies. Nothing less than capitalism itself was at stake, and the capitalist class always recognizes this threat, even though countless social commentators regularly succumb to the illusory hyperbole of "free and democratic" societies to this day. Thus, when the minimum wage laws were first enacted in Canada, the schedules of the low-wage industries of the day served as the legislative guide. When the federal unemployment relief plan was institutionalized, the "poor laws" of Britain provided the sense of measure. When social programs were institutionalized, assistance levels were set to insure that able-bodied workers would always be driven back into the workforce. When Order in Council P.C. 1003 rendered unions legal in 1944, the compliance of the labour movement with the general goals of capital was widely thought to be a sure bet. Highfalutin social ideals are intuited by the powers-that-be in capitalist societies as afflictions bound to create accumulation crises, as utopian lust sure to doom the wealthy and the privileged.

And so the early post-World War II gains of the labour movement were modest in scope and achievement. But this restrictive Fordist regime, designed to protect the integrity of capitalist social relations more than anything else, still proved to be too much for the capitalist class by the early 1970s. The corporate world came to the conclusion that labour needed to be chastened, and the push to abrogate the Fordist compact unilaterally was afoot.

The Rise of Neoliberalism

By the early 1970s capital could no longer live with the Fordist compromise. Within a few years the world of capitalist accumulation had taken on a new outlook, which has invariably framed policy changes in the last three decades. Since so much of the Fordist saw-off was entrenched institutionally, the neoliberal rollback has been a complicated, drawn-out development. The news has not been good for working people on the whole, nor was it ever meant to be.[20] Neoliberal conventions are about chiseling away at the modest working-class protections that largely defined the Fordist era.[21]

What prompted capital to reject the Fordist compact by the early 1970s? On the surface of capitalism's "golden age" things looked pretty good. Any tendencies towards crisis and instability were not visibly obvious. But "below the fold" factors were in play that would lead to a rejection of the post-war settlement by the business community. Capital could live with the compact as long as the rate of profit remained relatively high. This decisive condition is not easily manipulated by political strategies, especially in the short term, and for some it is an excellent example of the inevitable push of history that operates "behind our backs." From the mid-1940s to the mid-1960s, profit rates hovered between 15 and 20 percent in most economic sectors, although they were already displaying classic downward tendencies. By the latter part of the 1960s, the rate of profit took a noticeable hit. Accounts of the degree and scope of this sharp decline vary, but by the early 1970s all sectors of capital in all parts of the world had experienced dramatic profitability free-falls.[22] During the 1970s, profit rates reached their lowest point in the post-war era and were sometimes well into the single digits. The manufacturing sector in Canada was consistent with these worldwide trends.[23] Since the 1980s, there has been a modest recovery in the rates of profit but nothing matching the profitability heyday of the late 1940s.[24]

The capitalist class, especially its transnational faction, moved to restore its rates of profitability,[25] but even the modest protections of the Fordist era stood in its way. Capital became convinced that labour needed to be subdued. To put the matter more bluntly, the Fordist arrangements were quickly rejected as an optimal accumulation strategy. Capital was no longer willing to live with the grudging gains won by labour in the aftermath of World War II. This historic rejection of the post-war accords by capital initiated the "political economy of our adulthood." Our world feels so different when compared with the world of our parents and grandparents owing to a silent force of history — declining rates of profit — that led the capitalist class to declare steadfastly: "Enough! The deal is off!" Rising real wages, stagflation (high unemployment combined with high rates of inflation) and the militancy of labour during the 1970s only hardened the resolve of the business world to roll things back for the working class.

The strategy to rollback the Fordist accord has proceeded on two fronts. First, conventional productive practices have been extensively redesigned. Capital changed the contours of the shop-floor, restructured its network of production facilities, outsourced and sub-contracted, and reconfigured its labour force. Second, the Keynesian public policy paradigm was rejected. Neoliberal governments set about to restructure social programs, downsize, rationalize and privatize, all with a renewed emphasis on the promotion of "free markets." If the poster-theorist of Fordism was John Meynard Keynes, then the poster-theorist for the neoliberal era has been Milton Friedman.

Between the 1970s and the onset of crisis in 2008, Friedman's writings on monetarism, and the corresponding endorsement of free markets, were widely embraced. Neither figure was a friend of the working class, but Friedman's brand of contempt has been much more harmful for working people around the world.

Restructuring of Production

The restructuring of production — or what came to be called "flexible production" in some quarters — has proceeded in two complementary directions. Both strategies aimed to lower the overall cost of production by lowering wages. The first strategy focused on reorganizing the shop floor and is epitomized by the development of "lean production" schemes. This included workplace experimentation centred around the notions of teamwork, job rotation, worker-based quality control, multi-tasking and productive flexibility. This redesign of the shop floor has been championed by some as providing workers with greater degrees of control over the labour process and thus greater job satisfaction. Studies more sensitive to the plight of workers and relations of power have criticized lean production as a thinly veiled attempt to extract greater productivity out of working people.[26]

The second strategy is reflected in the plight of the Moores workers in Montreal. Transnational capital has been closing up shop in North America and moving operations to other parts of the world. The extent of plant closures in North America has been so extensive that the term "rust belt" entered our everyday lexicon. Sometimes capital closes factories only to re-open non-unionized facilities in a different region, state or province. More commonly, however, capital shifts its production southwards, where labour costs are significantly cheaper. Across the majority world, pools of impoverished people, often the victims of choreographed mass evictions from communally held property, are corralled into "below-subsistence" jobs. There has been a growth of export processing zones where the "autocracy" of capital rules much like it did in the nineteenth century. At the risk of being overly dramatic, Blake's "dark satanic mills" have resurfaced across the majority world. Nor is the resurrection of this old horror confined to the South. "Fly by night" factories, or "mushroom" factories, always characterized by poor pay and inhumane working conditions, operate below the radar screen in several North American cities and draw upon "illegal" migrant workers. Across the South, factory workers are paid a fraction of what their counterparts in the North typically receive, and the conditions of work are usually abysmal. Labour laws are poorly enforced, and any effort to organize workers is greeted with unrestrained hostility. The poorly paid, predominantly female workers of the South have little prospect of ever buying the goods they produce, with most of the product manufactured for retail markets in the minority world.

Although these strategies are often cloaked in business-friendly hyperbole, the basic goal is to drive down wages. A sort of "mobility logic" is intuited by all parties, and its disciplinary effects on labour have been staggering. As capital faces increasing competition from firms that have already availed themselves of cheaper labour in the South, they feel compelled to pull up stakes and join "the race to the bottom" to stay profitable and competitive. This is the sub-text to the closure of the Moores facility. In other sectors, especially those resource industries tied to the land and sea, firms have rationalized operations by closing plants. Obvious benefits accrue to those corporations that shift their production southwards to reduce their labour costs drastically. An equally important benefit indirectly accrues to capital in the North. In the face of widespread plant closures since the 1970s, the fear of God has been thrown into the working class.[27] As this mobility logic plays out, it augurs poorly for working people. Over the decades capital has been able to extract concessions from workers, who know that the prospect of sudden joblessness is very real. Across Canada, such bargaining under economic duress has zapped union strength, exacerbated tensions between labour leaders and the rank-and-file and contributed to the stagnation of real wages.

This restructuring is complemented by other corporate strategies that bear down negatively on the working class, especially by creating barriers to unionization. Many corporations have downsized their workforces aggressively and tried to hire as many non-unionized workers as possible. The more common division of working people into a core of elite employees with extensive professional training (usually in the natural sciences, engineering, accountancy, business administration and law) and a broader layer of unskilled direct producers still holds. But with each passing year in the neoliberal era, it is less likely that the "unskilled" workers of the world will be unionized. In the minority world unionization rates have been in decline, and unionized and non-unionized workers increasingly work alongside each other within the same firm. And across the majority world unionization is relatively rare.[28] Great lengths are taken to keep unions from forming in the world's export processing zones, and some countries have even taken political steps to insure that independent unions do not form. The repression of workers in the majority world also includes tactics like mass dismissals, beatings by corporate-hired thugs and the murder of union organizers and officials.

Large firms have shortened their supply contracts, a strategy that forces suppliers to take every measure necessary to keep wages down so that contracts can be rolled over at term. In some sectors, especially manufacturing, work is commonly outsourced to smaller firms, a discombobulating strategy from the standpoint of the working class that helps to keep the lid on union growth. Firms also increasingly contract out work, especially clerical and janitorial duties, to small-scale companies with high employee turnover. Such schemes help the larger company avoid disruptive labour struggles and helps lower overall costs. Most significantly, many larger firms simply sub-contract much of their production to smaller firms around the world. In some sectors of the economy, especially the apparel industry, such informal networks of production are characterized by layers of sub-contracting and a largely super-exploited female workforce. It has been widely observed that some of the world's most famous companies, like Nike, tend not to own factories. These larger firms never have much difficulty finding small-scale, local capitalists to meet their production needs. From the standpoint of the larger firms, the working class sort of disappears, at least in the sense that intractable labour problems are off-loaded to smaller companies. This broader network of global operations enjoys an overall advantage as it confronts a fractionated labour force that is rarely unionized. The benefits of outsourcing, contracting out and sub-contracting clearly belong to the corporate world, especially to the degree that the fluid, disaggregated workforce has a much harder time organizing and pressing for wage hikes.

In the last several decades these strategies have been embraced as "best corporate practices" by many businesses because they drive down wages. They also permit corporations to be more flexible when responding to evolving market conditions. In an era where markets are seen to be increasingly segmented, unpredictable and fickle, marketing executives now make last-minute assessments of "tastes" and implement production adjustments accordingly. The use of "small batch" and "just in time" production has become increasingly common, especially in the global apparel industry. These strategies have not displaced mass production by any stretch of the imagination; the neoliberal world is still dominated by assembly lines and mass consumption. Nevertheless, there have been greater efforts to match many goods and services to continually evolving consumer tastes and preferences.

On its own capital could only go so far. To complete the task of under-cutting workers and their wages capital pushed for a post-Keynesian public policy framework. It needed to reach the pools of cheap labour in the majority world without having to worry about things like tariffs, and it needed to create and exploit complementary pools of cheap labour in Canada without being troubled by unions. In a different language, capital needed to modify the economic structures of imperialism by loosening up international trading regulations, creating new opportunities for investment and bringing national policies in line with its revised accumulation strategies. In Canada this meant that the Keynesian policy framework of the Fordist era, a framework that simply provided too many protections and safeguards for workers, had to be tackled directly.

The Neoliberal Policy Paradigm

As the moniker implies, the essence of neoliberalism involved a return to classical liberal economic ideals of the nineteenth century, particularly regarding free markets. One helpful way to cut into the neoliberal policy paradigm is to consider its three leading ideological themes: free marketism, state indebtedness and corporate efficiency. Free marketism is the notion that unencumbered markets, that is, markets free from too much government regulation and interference, promote overall social well-being. In this view, free markets create efficiency, and they are the panacea for all social problems. Ultimately, the benefits of free markets "trickle down" to all. The notion of state indebtedness considers state debt to be generally a bad thing: it irresponsibly mortgages the future of a country, and politicians need to spend responsibly by refusing to run annual deficits. In the Canadian context, concern about running balanced budgets in the early 1990s was so intense that a debt-struck, accumulation-grubbing agency like the International Monetary Fund felt it necessary to cite the federal government for being too preoccupied with national indebtedness and neglecting such problems as unemployment. Corporate efficiency refers to the idea that corporations are naturally "lean" and "mean," that they are the most adept organizations when it comes to economic enterprise. It is held that corporations are naturally "flexible" and "responsive" to changing market conditions. The political corollary of this view is that governments are wasteful and inefficient and tend to "blow" taxpayer money in a way that contributes to overall economic sluggishness.

Each of these three ideological leitmotifs converge to drive home an oft-repeated mantra of neoliberalism: stateinvolvementintheeconomyisabadthing — averyverybadthing. The post-war Keynesian paradigm had sanctioned government intervention in the economy; neoliberalism, in stark contrast, has been anti-statist, or anti-dirigiste, to the core. This motif provides a rationalizing baseline for the panoply of neoliberal policies including deregulation, privatization, government downsizing, tax cuts, the corporatization of remaining Crown corporations (forcing state corporations to function like private companies with respect to service delivery and cost recovery), public-private partnerships and the extensive restructuring of social services. The confluence of these themes also helps to explain the shift from Keynesian "demand-side" economics to neoliberal "supply-side" economics. The Keynesian model sought to manage the economy by influencing the overall *demand* for goods and services, whereas neoliberal policies seek to stimulate the economy (the *supply* of goods and services) by lowering taxes and controlling the supply of money (monetarism).

A number of nationally based, corporate-funded think-tanks rose to prominence in the last few decades to hammer home these neoliberal themes, and they complement global agencies like the International Monetary Fund and the World Bank that have promoted the Washington Consensus at the policy level. In Canada these corporate-funded ideological factories include the Vancouver-based Fraser Institute, the Toronto-based C.D. Howe Institute and the Halifax-based Atlantic Institute for Market Studies (AIMS). Each Canadian centre has its ideological counterpart in the United States. The extreme right-wingism of the Fraser Institute is similar to that of the Heritage Foundation and the Cato Institute south of the border (the latter organization has sometimes accused the IMF of meddling too much in markets). The somewhat more moderate AIMS and the slightly more progressive C.D. Howe Institute are not unlike the US-based Institute for International Economics and the American Enterprise Institute. The powerful Council of Chief Executive Officers in Canada (formerly the Business Council on National Issues [BCNI]) also promotes neoliberal policies relentlessly, as does its counterpart in the United States, the Business Roundtable. Invariably, these "think-tanks" promote neoliberal policies (this is what they are funded to do) using the dominant ideological motifs of the age. With the onset of crisis in the fall of 2008 and the selective repudiation of neoliberalism at the rhetorical level, these agencies will have to reinvent themselves. They will, of course, ultimately say what their corporate backers ask them to say.

It matters very little that the ideological motifs of the neoliberal era maximize the gulf between "that which is rhetorically claimed" and "that which is really believed and practised." Evangelical support for free markets, for example, does not correspond to the real world, where commonplace corporate practices such as monopolies, oligopolies, interlocking corporate directorships, holding companies, protectionist demands, intra-firm trading and so on show that capital does its best to avoid "free" markets whenever the circumstances permit. Nor is there much good reason to believe that private capital is more efficient than state enterprise. Studies on the costs of health care in particular have shown that "private delivery" is woefully inefficient, and infamous cases of corporate waste sometimes make headlines. Nor is the hyped-up concern about government debt really all that well grounded, particularly given the centrality of credit in the process of accumulation, the undulating character of state debt, the decisive relationship between debt and the overall size of the economy and the cause of Canada's debt (largely corporate tax deferrals and interest charges and *not* "runaway government spending"). Indeed, the shallowness of the corporate world's concern about debt was revealed when the 2008 downturn prompted calls for massive increases in government spending irrespective of its effect on the country's fiscal ledger.

At a minimum, these foundational ideological themes are disingenuous and probably not widely believed by less gullible political or corporate leaders. But they do provide an ideological gloss for the neoliberal con-job, sucking in enough politicians and voters along the way. They have done their part to promote the gaseous consensus that permitted the piranha-like feeding-frenzy on Fordist institutions, particularly the ones providing modest protections for the working class. More to the political point, these themes promoted an ideological rejection of the Keynesian welfare state insofar as its programs empowered the working class. Not surprisingly, the neoliberal framework has been deployed selectively. Keynesian residues like high taxes continued to be the norm throughout the neoliberal era, as did extensive state props for corporation accumulation, especially in the area of military spending. Nevertheless, many prominent policy changes have successfully created the climate of austerity, helping to drive workers into "bad" jobs and making them less inclined, and less able, to unionize. The neoliberal agenda deliberately set the working class back on its heels without turning off state support for capital's accumulation strategies. These ideological themes of neoliberalism — free marketism and the celebration of corporate efficiency and debt hysteria — provided the ideological cannon fodder in the capitalist class's assault on the Canadian working class between the 1970s and the onset of crisis in the fall of 2008.

Three specific baskets of neo-liberal policies can be identified. First, liberalized trading regimes, unencumbered by government regulation and tariffs, were expanded. The signature of the neoliberal era was the North American Free Trade Agreement (NAFTA). A closely related set of policies pushed de-regulation and privatization, especially in the telecommunications, utilities and transportation sectors. The second set of policies altered and scaled back social programs. The notion of "restructuring" social programs, always cloaked in the language of "reducing costs" and "improving client delivery," came into fashion in the 1980s and 1990s. Some social programs were cut entirely, while most faced extensive redesign and alteration. At the federal level there was extensive reform to the Employment Insurance system and the cessation of the Canada Assistance Plan in 1995. At the provincial level, reforms included the tightening of eligibility requirements and alterations to the scope of social assistance programs. The third cluster of neoliberal policies took aim at working people directly, with the provinces usually taking the lead. They include a relaxation of provincial labour codes, restrictive policies regarding the minimum wage, a greater tendency to resort to back-to-work legislation and broadening the definition of "essential service."

Each basket of neoliberal policies has a *downward wage logic* at its core. First, the unfettering of economies, including the liberalization of trade, privatization, public-private partnerships, government downsizing and the corporatization of state operations has the deliberate effect of weakening or smashing unions and forcing bargaining concessions. Second, reforms to social programs are designed to drive workers into low-wage jobs and keep them there as long as possible. As working people breathe in the heavy air of neoliberal austerity they are more likely to calculate that it is better to persevere through a rotten job, with rotten pay and rotten working conditions, rather than suffer the indignity of joblessness and endure the harsh alternative provided by gutted social assistance programs. Of capitalism it could be said that the threat of starvation is lorded over the head of every worker, and of neoliberalism it could be said that this threat is never trivialized. Third, the neoliberal policies that target workers directly, especially those attacking the principle and practice of unionization, have made it much more difficult for the working class to organize and press for better wages. Again, the overall advantage goes to employers, who can more easily confront efforts to organize secure in the knowledge that the laws of the land are once again stacked in their favour. Large and small enterprises in both the public and private sphere are comforted by the fact that they can hold the line on wages without having to worry too much about working-class oomph.

In the neoliberal era things got worse for working people. As observed above, this is not to suggest that the Fordist world was terribly generous. In matters of public policy the state rule has always been blunt: Refrain! Restrain! Contain! The left in Canada could be gently chastised for losing perspective on the grudging nature of the concessions made by capital in the middle phase of the twentieth century, especially those inclined to view the early post-World War II decades as the "gold standard" of social policy. But things are worse now. The achievements of labour are now used to brow-beat working people. The progressive residues of the post-war policy agenda have been purged. Without historical compunction neoliberal politicians routinely use long-standing social policies as weapons in the assault on the working class. Social assistance programs, for example, have been re-named to remind all Canadians that no-one should expect "handouts" from the state and explicitly restructured to force welfare recipients into the workforce (or to guilt them into finding alternative ways of surviving). Things got so bad that the term "poornography" arose in some quarters of the progressive community to describe both the dispiriting character of the restructured social assistance programs and the rhetoric of those "common-sense" neoliberal politicians who pushed for changes. Similarly, provincial minimum wage regulations have been used to promote the stagnation of real wages across Canada since the early 1980s. And in classic Orwellian fashion the old pogey system was renamed to emphasize "work" rather than unemployment, and its gutting caused all Canadians to lose confidence in prospective unemployment relief. When tallied up these reforms remind all workers that the only virtuous mode of existence nowadays is to "seek and keep" work at all cost. And should working people be so inclined to improve their lot by organizing, labour laws have frequently been reformed to quash spontaneous solidarity, trim any instinct for protest or defiance and generally undermine workers' capacity for collective resistance.

Table 1.2 outlines the basic features of neoliberalism, some of which are examined in greater detail in the following chapters. Although the richness of cultural transitions warrants more attention than is offered here, some aspects of neoliberal culture can be highlighted. There has been the gradual ascendancy of a culture inclined to judge striking workers and the poor harshly. Of the neoliberal era it is sometimes said that the "war on poverty" gave way to a "war on the poor." The last few decades have sometimes been summarized as the "age of falling expectations," an expression that captures the sense of many young people, who no longer expect their lives to be better than the lives of their parents.[29] Working people are assailed with the idea that the key to their well-being is to consume in accordance with their "individuality." The indiscriminating "mass consumption" of Fordism has ceded ground to "narcissistic mass consumption" in the neoliberal era — buying stuff as the

Table 1.2 The Neoliberal Regime, from the Early 1970s to the Present

Production Conventions	Prevailing Policy Framework	Salient Cultural Features
• Development of "flexible" production methods tailored to latest consumer tastes	• Ideological ascendency of "free marketism" • Elevation of concern about government debt	• Ascendency of culture of harsh judgment, especially "poor bashing"
• Widespread corporate relocation and restructuring	• Cultivation of a climate of economic austerity	• Age of "falling expectations" • Intensified commodification of "well-being" (selling the "good life" by selling products and services)
• Extensive corporate use of sub-contracting and short-term contracting	• Rationalization and contraction of government services • Widespead privatization and deregulation	
• Redoubled efforts to articulate production with increasingly segmented markets	• Restructuring of established social programs at federal and provincial levels	• Deepening of market segmentation and stratification • Cultivation of the notion of the "flexible" worker and emerging cultural recognition of the "non-standard workday"
• Growing prominence of "financial" and "transnational" capital	• Clawbacks to the Fordist labour regime	

key to being special, unique and beautiful. In the last decade consumption has also been pushed as the "key to freedom." North Americans were told to consume to combat the "war on terror," an almost surreal message when contrasted with the "kitchen gardens" and rationing of World War II. A placard at an anti-war rally in March 2003 captured much of the spirit of the neoliberal era in an uncanny way: "Consume. Consume. Bomb. Bomb. Consume. Consume." And most importantly, working people are reminded constantly that unions cannot be guaranteed to solve their problems, but that hard work, adaptability, flexibility and stoicism in the workplace will invariably prove to be beneficial.

Over the last four decades the pillars of Fordism eroded. This dismantling of the post-war order, perhaps better referred to as a unilateral amendment by capital, is not all that surprising. It is helpful to stand back a little and reflect on the inevitable fate that awaits any compact between capital and labour over the longer term. For its part, capital can never rest content with the prevailing political order owing to the press of economic factors largely beyond its control. Capitalism is unsettling by its very nature. Its immanent tendency towards crisis is never really beaten, although there can be periods of relative prosperity and optimism. As the years pass and as concerns about profits gather, the framework that governs the specific conflicts between capital and labour, especially those pertaining to wages, unions and general worker protections, will be subject, of necessity, to renegotiation. From the standpoint of working people who thought that previous triumphs of the labour movement were secure, the changes seem unthinkable. The onset of a profitability crisis in the early 1970s threw the contradictions of Fordism into relief for capital. The pillars of the Fordist regime gave the working class modest protections, and capital had to take a run at those pillars to respond to the profitability crisis. A *modus vivendi* between capital and labour is possible over the short-term, as we saw for some of the post-war period in Canada, but the very character of capitalism's *modus operandi* renders a long-lasting accord between capital and working people improbable. Time is bound to erode all capitalist compacts, and hence the mistake of the Canadian left might be said to have been its faith in the possibility of a lasting "compromise" between capital and labour. A century of struggle yielded the Fordist compact, but it was scratched in sand, not etched in stone. No compact in capitalist society will endure, and recent decades have amply demonstrated this impossibility, much to the left's collective grief. The Fordist compromise of the early post-World War II era was followed, quite expectedly, by the neoliberal rollback of the last several decades.

After Neoliberalism

This book highlights aspects of the attack on the working class over the neoliberal era. Chapter 2 looks at the altered conceptions of the ideal worker and the deregulation of labour law. Chapter 3 examines the declining rates of unionization, the falling incidence of worker militancy and the stagnation of real wages. Chapter 4 looks at the character of the politics of the minimum wage and the extent of the low-wage sphere. Chapter 5 surveys the evolving unemployment relief program and the decline in welfare incomes.

Neoliberalism has been the undeclared attack by the capitalist class against the working class. Over the years it has taken its toll on both working people and the left. As neoliberalism passes, or as elements of its ideological infrastructure are repudiated, owing to the onset of crisis in 2008, it is not the case that things are about to get better for working people. The devil is in the practice, not in the ideological gloss. Another great compromise is not in the offing; the pendulum is not about to swing back any time soon. Accordingly, the last chapter offers an assessment of the left in Canada and discusses strategies to revive a left culture and reverse the fortunes of the working class.

Notes

1. Men's Wearhouse quotes drawn from <http://www.menswearhouse.com/aboutus/our_community/giving_back.jsp?FOLDER%3C%3Efolder_id=25343 7430240081 1&n1=About+Us&n2=Our+Business&n3=Our+Philosophy&bmUI D=1206462044109>. Last accessed March 24, 2008.

2. Quote and the following financial information extracted from *Men's Wearhouse 2006 Annual Report.* Accessed at <http://library.corporate-ir.net/library/10/109/109554/items/246497/MensWearhouse2006AR.pdf>. Last accessed March 24, 2008.

3. Mike King, "Eighth Time Unlucky for Couple," *Montreal Gazette*, February 29, 2008. Accessed at <http://www.canada.com/montrealgazette/news/business/story.html?id=4a0d9cd1-15e1-4308-89c3-d7883f6b81ce>. Last accessed March 24, 2008.

4. Quotes by workers at Golden Brand factory from <http://www.ourjobsmatter.org/>. Blog established by the North American apparel industry's Union Needletrades, Industrial and Textile Employees/ Hotel Employees and Restaurant Employees (UNITE HERE). Last accessed March 24, 2008.

5. See Press Release, April 19, 2008, UNITE HERE. Accessed at <http://www.unitehere.org/presscenter/release.php?ID=3478>. Last Accessed July 1, 2008.

6. See part of UNITE HERE's e-Activist postings at <http://action.unitehere.org/campaign/goldenbrandfactory>. Last Accessed July 1, 2008.

7. See UNITE HERE press release of May 9, 2008, at <http://www.unitehere.ca/pages/releasedetail.php?press_id=185>. Last accessed July 1, 2008.

8. See <http://www.canada.com/montrealgazette/news/business/story.html?id=863c4223-7042-4cb1-8fe6-f7ce2c3dc3e6>. Last Accessed July 1, 2008.

9. A survey of the analytical dimensions of either term in the Canadian context is beyond the compass of this study, as is an exploration of the theories themselves.

The formative works regarding "regimes of accumulation" are Michel Aglietta, *A Theory of Capitalist Regulation* (London: Verso, 1987) and Alain Lipietz, *Mirages and Miracles: The Crises of Global Fordism*, (London: Verso,1987). Insofar as these writers emphasize the endogenous crisis tendencies of capitalist accumulation I find their work illuminating and persuasive. The term "social structure of accumulation" draws heavily on analyses like the work of David Gordon, "Stages of Accumulation and Long Economic Cycles," in Terence K. Hopkins and Immanuel Wallerstein, eds., *Processes of the World System* (Beverly Hills: Sage Publications, 1980) and Samuel Bowles, "Power and Profits: The Social Structure of Accumulation and the Profitability of the Postwar U.S. Economy," *Review of Radical Political Economics*, Vol. 18, No. 1-2, 132-167 (1986). Insofar as their work emphasizes the relationship between institutions and class struggle I find it equally helpful. A thoughtful and schematic comparative essay of both schools of thought can be found in David M. Kotz, "The Regulation Theory and the Social Structure of Accumulation Approach," in *Social Structures of Accumulation: The Political Economy of Growth and Crisis*, eds. David M. Kotz, Terrence McDonough and Michael Reich (Cambridge University Press, 1994).

10. It is the institutional emphasis of both regulation theory and social structure of accumulation theory that provides the academic cushion for this chapter's presentation, although I have separated out three relevant spheres for consideration in terms of their proximity to the transubstantiation of value: production (including the labour process), public policy and culture. And ever since Gramsci the term "Fordism" is just too alluring and widely used to avoid. I regard both schools as a much needed counter to liberal academic instincts that typically fail to ground the analysis of institutions in the social relations of power or in the immanent tendencies of capitalist production and accumulation. The reifying instinct of liberal scholarship may very well help it dodge the charge of "economism" or "reductionism," but such pleasures of liberal orthodoxy to others remains a mystery. Two recent contributions to the social structure of accumulation theory give a good indication of its efforts to connect institutions and their development with class struggle and other contradictions endemic to capitalist economies. On the stabilization of contradictions and the call for a circumscribed use of the term, see Martin Wolfson, "Neo-liberalism and the Social Structure of Accumulation," *Review of Radical Political Economics* 35: 3 (Summer 2003), pp. 255–62. A general survey can be found in Terrence McDonough, "Social Structures of Accumulation Theory: The State of the Art," *Review of Radical Political Economics* 40: 2 (Spring 2008), pp. 153–73.

11. Ever since Nietzsche led the revolt against metaphysics and philosophy, a revolt that culminated in the anti-essentialism of much twentieth-century social philosophy, especially in the writings of the progressive American philosopher Richard Rorty, the analytical richness of Marxist orthodoxy has had a rough go of it (numbering among the low points for me was Leszek Kolakowski's triumphant identification of the labour theory of value as a mere ideological construction in his *Main Currents of Marxism*). Insofar as this study finds Marx's distinctions between "essential social relations" and "phenomenal social relations" helpful and in accordance with a much maligned notion of what science should even be, and to the extent that it carries such sensibilities forward to help make sense of "the world that stands before us" today, I should at least point out that it is not in step with the analytical predilections of the age.

12. Kotz's identification of regulation theory and social structure of accumulation theory as "theories of the intermediate run" seems helpful enough. Of course, to

28

any students of capitalist history, especially those convinced that this kind of society is hopelessly alienating and ultimately untenable to we humans, it is the relationship between the intermediate run and the long run that is the real hub of the matter, especially the capacity of the "intermediate run" to parry capitalism's "tendencies" and enhance the resiliency of capitalist social formations.

13. William K. Carrol, "From Canadian Corporate Elite to Transnational Capitalist Class: Transitions in the Organization of Corporate Power," *The Canadian Review of Sociology and Anthropology* 44: 3 (August 2007), p. 268.

14. James W. Rinehart's *The Tyranny of Work: Alienation and the Labour Process*, 5th ed. (Toronto: Thomson Nelson, 2006) continues to be the best survey of these developments in the Canadian context. The discussion is organized around Marx's theory of estranged labour. It integrates historical developments with contemporary critiques of neoliberal strategies, and there are many good reasons explaining why the work has passed through several editions.

15. As Allan Greer wrote in a discussion on the origins of the capitalist labour market in Canada: "Today, family farms in the 'advanced' nations are subordinated to a capitalist system to which they must adapt; in the early nineteenth century it was the other way round: capitalist enterprise had to adapt itself to the prevailing non-capitalist environment." "Wage Labour and the Transition to Capitalism: A Critique of Pentland," *Labour/Le Travail* 15 (Spring 1985), p. 20.

16. In recent decades a growing body of literature has analytically filled in the development of capitalist social relations in Canada. The best survey of these developments from the standpoint of the working class continues to be Bryan D. Palmer's *Working Class Experience: Rethinking the History of Canadian Labour, 1800–1991*, 2nd ed. (Toronto: McClelland and Stewart Inc., 1992). See also Craig Heron, *The Canadian Labour Movement: A Short History*, 2nd ed. (Toronto: James Lorimer, 1996), particularly the pre-World War II chapters. This growing body of literature has created an analytical momentum that permits the appearance of excellent "second generation" collections like Laurel Sefton MacDowell and Ian Radforth's *Canadian Working Class History: Selected Readings*, 2nd ed. (Toronto: Canadian Scholars Press, 2000).

17. Sometimes the formation of this class was almost comical, and we would laugh were it not for the fact that they were miscreants lacking any compunction whatsoever. See Gustavus Myers, *A History of Canadian Wealth*, v.1 (Toronto: J. Lewis & Samuel, 1972).

18. The earliest study to speak to these trends was H. Clare Pentland's groundbreaking "The Development of a Capitalistic Labour Market in Canada," *Canadian Journal of Economics and Political Science* 25 (1959), pp. 450–61.

19. It is important to stress the grudging nature of Fordism from the standpoint of capital. In this spirit see Richard McIntyre and Michael Hillard, "The 'Limited Capital-Labour Accord': May it Rest in Peace," *Review of Radical Political Economics* 40: 3 (Summer 2008), pp. 244–49.

20. It is quite appropriate to refer to this assault as a war. See James Laxer, *The Undeclared War: Class Conflict in the Age of Cyber Capitalism* (Toronto: Penguin Books, 1999).

21. There are four bodies of literature on neoliberalism including analytic reviews, analytically focused studies on its specific problems, analytic accounts and non-analytic descriptions of its various problems. Good examples of the analytic reviews includes Gérard Duménil and Dominique Lévy, "The Economics of US Imperialism at the turn of the 21st Century," *Review of International Political Economy* 11: 4 (October 2004), pp. 657–76, and Vincent Navarro, "The Worldwide Class Struggle," *Monthly Review*

58: 4 (September 2006), pp. 18–33. An example of the second body of literature is Robin Blackburn, "The Subprime Crisis," *New Left Review* 50 (March/April 2008), pp. 63–106. The third kind of writing includes the social structure of accumulation and regulation theory literature referred to in notes 9 and 10. An example of the non-analytic studies is Steven High, *Industrial Sunset: The Making of North America's Rust Belt, 1969–1984* (Toronto: University of Toronto Press, 2003). There is a fifth body of literature that might be dubbed "journalistic accounts" or "neoliberal kiss-and-tells." An example of this gumshoeing is John Perkins, *Confessions of an Economic Hit-Man* (New York: Plume, 2006).

22. A solid summary of this account focusing on profit decline can be found in Fred Moseley, "The United States Economy at the Turn of the Century: Entering a New Era of Prosperity," *Capital and Class* 67 (Spring 1999), pp. 25–45.

23. M.J. Webber and D.L. Rigby, "The Rate of Profit in Canadian Manufacturing, 1950–1981," *Review of Radical Political Economics* 18: 1 & 2 (1986), pp. 33–55. The authors conclude that the average annual rate of profit of the manufacturing sector in Canada went from 45 percent in the early 1950s to 28 percent by 1981, a 17 percent decline.

24. According to Gérard Duménil and Dominique Lévy, the rate of recovery of the rate of profit since the 1980s in the United States has only been about one half of its early post-war levels. "The Profit Rate: Where and How Much Did It Fall? Did it Recover? (USA 1948–2000)," *Review of Radical Political Economics* 34 (2002), pp. 437–61.

25. One of the leading proponents of the rising influence of transnational capital is William I. Robinson in *A Theory of Global Capitalism: Production, Class, and State in a Transnational World* (Baltimore: The Johns Hopkins University Press, 2004). See also Leslie Sklair, *The Transnationalist Capitalist Class* (Malden, MA: Blackwell Publishers Inc., 2001). On the influence of transnational capital in the Canadian context see David Langille's "The Business Council on National Issues and the Canadian State," *Studies in Political Economy* 24 (Autumn, 1987).

26. See James Rinehart, "Transcending Taylorism and Fordism? Two Decades of Work Restructuring," in *Work, Difference and Social Change: Two Decades after Braverman's Labour and Monopoly Capital.* (Conference Proceedings, State University of New York, Binghamton, New York, May 8–10, 1998).

27. See the collection of articles in Henk Thomas, ed., *Globalization and Third World Trade Unions: The Challenge of Rapid Economic Change* (London: Zed Books, 1995).

28. A readable review of this outlook from the standpoint of working people is Jamie Swift's *Wheel of Fortune: Work and Life in the Age of Falling Expectations* (Toronto: Between the Lines, 1995).

2

Conceptions of Working Life and Labour Law

On Wednesday, December 27, 2006, just before Canadians were about to ring in the New Year, the *Globe and Mail* ran an article in its business section on the job prospects for working people. Entitled "Workers May Have Reasons to Cheer in 2007," the piece claimed that workers could expect "greater job security, fatter paycheques and a more diverse and flexible workplace in 2007."[1] The conclusions were drawn from a survey of more than two hundred managers conducted by an internet employment site called CareerBuilder.ca. The managers expressed concern about the tightening job market in Canada and predicted that they would have to offer better salaries and working conditions to attract prospective employees. They suggested that Canadian workers could expect to see offers of higher salaries, the re-hiring of retirees, a greater openness to flexible work arrangements and a willingness to take on less experienced workers. The article quoted the managing director of CareerBuilder: "The positive climate for job seekers will be challenging for hiring managers already coping with a shrinking labour pool as the baby boomer generation retires.... As employers struggle to stay competitive, Canadian workers will see higher salaries, more flexible work schedules and better career advancement opportunities in 2007." The piece expressed no concern about the narrowness of the survey, nor did it try to balance any of the conclusions about rosy hiring and employment trends with dissenting views. Canadian workers, its effusive tone led the reader to believe, had good reasons to be hopeful about the upcoming year.

Almost a year to the day later, the executive director of the Canadian Centre for Policy Alternatives issued a report assessing corporate performance and its consequences for working people in the aftermath of the Free Trade Agreement (FTA). Entitled *20 Years Later: Has Free Trade Delivered on Its Promise?* the CCPA brief observed that many of the companies that had pushed for the FTA had made substantial job cuts despite promises of prosperity. Twenty-eight of the 150 or so BCNI (Business Council on National Issues) corporations had seen their revenues rise by $93 billion but over the same period had reduced their combined workforce by more than 200,000 employees. The report also noted that while the payrolls of Canadian CEOs had ballooned the incomes of most Canadians had stagnated or declined. Its conclusions were unequivocal: "The vast majority of Canadians have not prospered in the free trade era. The vast majority, despite working harder, have experienced either marginal income gains, none at all, or have seen their real incomes lose ground. Many are working harder just to keep what they have. Others are falling behind."[2]

When it comes to the economy, it is not unusual to encounter both positive and negative reports about particular issues. In 2007 some working people would have been able to secure decent remuneration, others would have received pink slips after years of loyal service, and still others would have had difficulty making ends meet. But even when taken together, such reports provide little account of the realities that bear down on working people. Critical assessment must move beyond the mere expression of *something good* or *something bad* about economic matters. Discussions must be framed within the context of the evolving dynamics of productive life in capitalist society, and especially the crises these dynamics engender, including the harmful consequences for working people. Clearly, the *Globe and Mail* article is a journalistic fluff-piece and the CCPA report contains important anecdotal and research evidence, but neither piece provides even a hint of the socio-economic forces in play over the last thirty years.

The condition of working people has been deteriorating, and this deterioration is a central goal of the neoliberal accumulation project, not merely collateral harm emerging in the face of globalization. To gain a better sense of this direct assault it is helpful to distinguish between, on the one hand, working people who are partially protected from both the whims of managers and the exigencies of capital accumulation and, on the other, those who are much more vulnerable. Typically, vulnerability is lessened by things like belonging to a union and strong labour laws. For example, simple union membership is associated with noticeably higher wages.[3] Jeffery Harrod's study of vulnerable workers in the world economy gives a useful distinction between *established* and *unprotected* workers:

> The division between the unprotected worker and the established worker, as with all relations based on power, is one of degree and is open to dispute. At the ends of the extreme, however, the situation is very clear. In the bipartite social relations of the auto industry in the United States in the 1970s… the bulk of the workers were protected from dismissal for life, surrounded by laws, practices, and constraints against employer's power… [At the other end of the spectrum is] the casual worker in a third-world city who is at the mercy of the casual employer of labour and can never expect the state, union, or other worker organizations to prevent the most dire economic and physical abuse.[4]

Harrod reminds us that this distinction between the established worker (also called the Fordist worker in this book) and the unprotected worker (also called the neoliberal worker) is more difficult to maintain as we pull away from the extremes. Nevertheless, it is useful to organize our discussion around these two types. The working class is characterized by an ever-changing ratio between established workers and unprotected workers. To put this in colloquial terms, there has always been a split in the workforce between "good" jobs, with the features of the established worker, and "bad" jobs, with the vulnerabilities of the unprotected worker. This segmentation tends to hold irrespective of levels of education and even professional background. Much of the neoliberal agenda can be thought of as an attempt to change this balance of "good" and "bad" jobs so that the latter faction of the working class becomes even more commonplace. The focus of this chapter is the assault on the Fordist or established worker at the level of popular conceptions of work and through labour law.

To emphasize the helpfulness of this distinction between established and unprotected workers, we can draw a comparison with discussions about growing income inequality in Canada and elsewhere. Income gaps and inequality have worsened in recent decades; the rich, we are often told, are getting richer, and the poor, somewhat predictably, are getting poorer. A well-publicized study by the Organisation for Economic Co-operation and Development (OECD) in 2008 entitled *Growing Unequal? Income Distribution and Poverty in OECD Countries*, for example, found that Canada's level of income inequality exceeded the OECD average and that this level had widened in the last decade.[5] Although the focus on growing income inequality helps counter neoliberal boasts about "rising tides" and "downward trickles," it does not clarify the manner in which social relations of power are played out for those who, simply put, must work to eat. Rather, such discussions confirm that something is terribly wrong and getting worse by the year but provide few insights into the attack on working people. To this problem we must add the nagging feeling that these discussions suggest that capitalism was considerably more equal in the past, an untruth that greatly exaggerates the modest degree of income re-distribution in the early post-World War II decades.[6] These concerns are compounded by the fuzzy analytical status of growing income inequality: Is it a "goal" of the wealthy and thus, in a sense, a "cause" of neoliberalism, or is it merely a "symptom" of altered accumulation strategies?[7] And of far greater concern is the fact that what really matters is the assault that transpires inside the cohort that is "getting poorer." A focus on income levels does not begin to address many of the class dynamics central to neoliberalism. A worker making $25,000 a year and another making $90,000 might experience neoliberalism in a similar way if neither is protected by a union. Two workers each making $70,000 a year might experience neoliberalism in a vastly different way if one of them lives in a province where labour standards legislation has been gutted and workplace resistance significantly weakened. And income inequality measures tell us nothing about Canadian women's hourly wages, which tend to hover much closer to the minimum wage than those of their male counterparts. In short, the study of income levels and income inequality does not take analysis very far. Critical discussion must strive to get to the social relations of power at the heart of working life, and the distinction between the established worker and the unprotected worker can help to focus on the changing vulnerabilities endemic to working life, the constant struggles over wages and the shifting capacities for collective resistance.

The distinction between the Fordist worker and the neoliberal worker requires the use of economic indicators that do not typically dominate the nightly news, which tends to reference such items as interest rates, exchange rates, inflation rates, GDP growth, stock market quotes and commodity prices. These commonplace statistical data are unhelpful in our analysis for at least three important reasons. First, they establish a way of speaking about our productive world that is aloof from the social relations of power that frame so much workplace conflict, particularly racial, class and gender struggles. Second, the prevailing statistical representations of economic life fail to touch upon the vulnerabilities working people *feel* inside the workplace. And finally, this way of speaking about economic matters fails to let us see how workers personally strategize to pay bills, raise a family, keep a job and generally make ends meet. The eulogists of capitalist society typically leave the commonplace liberal discourse about productive life unexamined for political and ideological reasons, but a healthy suspicion towards this familiar lexical universe must be maintained. Capturing something about "the economy" — itself a monstrously abstract concept with a seemingly insatiable appetite for human beings — is not quite the same as capturing something about the struggles and well-being of working people as they produce commodities. As the philosopher Hegel reminded us long ago, reflection is most impaired when abstract discussions fail to have a robust concrete residue, and the economic indicators that constitute the nightly news amount to a sort of habitual dodge that keeps the focus off of the real struggles and anxieties that so many working people face so much of the time.

In contrast, the indicators discussed in the following chapters help us gain an insight into the struggles of working people in the neoliberal era. The Fordist worker was shielded with an array of protections ranging from unions to labour laws. In the post-war era, working people *thought* about working life in a manner that affirmed these protections, especially with respect to unions and unionization. And, predictably, with these protections, real wages rose appreciably over the course of the first three post-war decades. It is these pillars of the established or Fordist worker that have been assailed. Neoliberalism is about getting to this worker by undermining the salient protections of the Fordist era, especially unions. In the process, the dominant set of ideas about working life, especially those that affirmed the importance of unions, have been culturally re-worked, sometimes bluntly and sometimes in more subtle ways. The understandings about work and working life have, in effect, been refigured in the social imagination. Thinking poorly of unions, in particular, has come to be something of a national pastime. At the same time, legal developments have aimed at insuring that the ranks of the Fordist worker dwindle while the ranks of the neoliberal worker grow. These trends are the focus of this chapter. The next chapter discusses declining rates of unionization, the drop in labour militancy and the stagnation in real wages.

The Shifting Notion of Working Life

Part of the assault on the Fordist worker has been waged at the level of the social imagination, or what academics call the "social discourse about work-ing life" or the "intersubjective consciousness regarding work." In the early post-World War II period a certain notion of working life more or less lodged itself in everyone's noodle. A working person toiled around forty hours each week, grabbed a little overtime here and there, could reasonably count on a decent wage to raise a family and could tuck a little money away with the hope of sending children to college. These ideas were encumbered with lots of patriarchal baggage about "manly work" and the importance of "bread-winners" to be sure, notions that persisted even as women were drawn back into the post-war workforce. But it was also understood, most critically, that a worker could proudly belong to a union and that his or her identity was quite separate from managers and the owners of firms. Conflict between labour and management was regarded as a normal feature of life. Unions, worker solidarity, strong labour laws and the occasional strike all served important purposes and were not seen as undermining the prosperity of society. To these social understandings it should also be added that the typical worker expected to be employed at the same place for a lifetime unless the desire "to change jobs" arose. And in the event of a brief spell of joblessness a worker had faith that government programs like federal Unemployment Insurance would smooth out the transition between seasons or between jobs.

Such were the social understandings about work and working life that typified the Fordist era, understandings essentially imbued with the central idea that workers were to be shielded from the ravages of capitalist labour markets and the caprice of employers. This cultural notion of working life reflected real-working-life experiences of the established or Fordist worker. All this has now changed. This notion has slowly given way to a conception of

35

working life more in tune with the accumulation imperatives of the neoliberal age. This newer notion took shape in public policy declarations, government papers, clips and stories in the news media, university studies and reports from business-friendly think-tanks. In recent decades a working person is much more likely to be regarded as someone who should be grateful for merely *having* a job, should be willing to work variable hours and longer hours if necessary, should be satisfied with prevailing wage rates, should see scrimping and saving as a virtue and should not expect too much in the way of immediate rewards for hard work. Most of all, a worker should be suspicious of the self-serving agendas of unions and wary of union membership. She should regard herself, ideally, as an "associate," someone who is part of a shared corporate quest for overall enrichment and success. In the neoliberal paradigm of working life the notion of "solidarity" has given way to the notion of "team work within the corporate or bureaucratic family," and confrontations leading to a work stoppage signal the absence of the virtue of compromise. Strikes, simply speaking, are passé. The new worker might expect to pass through several careers over the course of a lifetime and always be willing to acquire new "skill sets." To be a worker, it is sometimes said, is to "learn a living" just as much as it is to "earn a living." And, again in the jargon of the day, an unemployed worker must not expect a "hand out" from the government but rather a "hand up." It could be said that this new conception of a noble toiler is a blend of the "rugged individual" (who toughs it out without state assistance during the rough times), the "virtuous ascetic" (who expects little and is willing to make do with less) and Ben Franklin's "industrious soul" (who is willing to work hard and long hours).

It is helpful to expand briefly on some of these elements of the new paradigm of working life, elements that invariably repudiate the idea that the workplace is confrontational or that unions are necessary. To begin, there is a widespread idea that the "old economy" has been left behind. This is manifested by a revealing language of rupture, or a decisive break with the past, whenever there is talk about the economy. At the heart of this lexical shift is the idea that the old economy, or the "traditional capitalist economy," has been supplanted by a new economy with essentially different dynamics. This view is as likely to be purveyed by social scientists as much as it is claimed by journalists, politicians and business leaders:

> Over the past several decades prominent social scientists have claimed that massive and qualitative structural changes have taken place in advanced capitalist nations. These changes are said to be so vast that concepts such as "industrial society" or "capitalist society" no longer capture the essence of the new social order. In their place, new terms have arisen, symbolic of the changing social

realities — the service society, the knowledge society, technotronic, post-capitalist society, and most commonly, post-industrial society. At the root of this transformation are technological advance and the consequent shift from an economy based on the production of goods to one centred around the provision of services.[8]

One corollary of this view is that the institutions of the old economy, especially unions, have outlived their usefulness. A revealing example of this widespread line of thought was evident in a commentary by Tony Comper, former CEO of the Bank of Montreal financial group. Comper expressly claimed that the hierarchical corporate structures that typified the past were being supplanted by new, non-hierarchical firms with fundamentally different workforce dynamics:

> Until 1996, when demographer David Foote published his best-sell-ing book *Boom, Bust and Echo*, I had not known that what I was doing was something he called "spiralling." And it had not yet occurred to me that spiralling — mixing lateral moves with promotions, switch-ing disciplines, acquiring new skill sets — would be pegged as the dominant "lifestyle" in an increasingly hierarchy-free 21st-century corporate work place. I do not just accept this turn of events, I revel in it. And when the process is complete at BMO, *the very notion of "bosses" and "workers" and a division between the two will have become a quaint memory of the Industrial Age*. In the new, *flattened corporate universe*, a manager is a member of a *team* — the one whose specific talents include facilitation, coordination, communication and inspiration. It is taken as a given that *all colleagues will treat the success of the organization as a matter of pride, self-interest and personal responsibility.*[9]

Just in case there was a bothersome concern that these ideas were associated with a socialized property form, Comper quickly added: "I am not going to claim that workers, in the modern guise of colleagues and associates, *have seized the means of production*. But the top-down corporate world I entered back in 1967 is *vanishing*, ever so quietly, *into the history books*."[10]

These shifting ideas about the heart and soul of the evolving "informa-tion" economy have intersected with the renewed emphasis on training and re-training in the last two decades, an intersection that adds to the erosion of the view that the workplace is inherently conflictual and that unions are inevitable. Government programs, media reports and university research initiatives across Canada make up what could be called "the training regime." The target of this renewed emphasis on skills training has been those workers displaced by decades of corporate restructuring, government employees, recipients of social assistance and the legion of casual workers. The purported goal has been to improve the overall skill level of the Canadian workforce generally and to match personal skills and know-how to the requirements of specific industries. This training regime has been significant in undermining the Fordist conception of work by de-politicizing the workplace. The worker is viewed as little more than a bearer of "skill sets," the workplace is set up as a place in need of unique skills and the broader economy is construed merely as a place where skill requirements are matched with skill levels. As well, the training regime tends to pit worker against worker, suggesting that a "leg up" in the economy will be found in the acquisition of new skills. The Canadian state in recent years went as far as encouraging workers to think of themselves as "Me Inc."[11] Working people are reminded that the focus must be on the "opportunity" created by re-training. It amounts to a return to the Victorian notion of self-help, with the implication that the real conflicts in society are not along class lines but rather between working people themselves. The training regime also contributes to the neoliberal idea of working life by emphasizing flexibility: a working person must be ready to adapt and re-tool. Manfred Bienefeld's incisive comments on the relationship between training and public calls for a flexible workforce are smack dab on: "Slogans like the need for 'permanent retraining' or for 'lifetime learning' are widely used to describe and justify the casualization of labour, which is creating a world in which workers are paid what it takes to get them to the factory gates each day, hoping the straw boss will give them the nod."[12]

The training regime encourages a technical view of the workplace, one that is consistent with the ideologically loaded claim that conflict and struggle are no longer necessary. The workplace is not "made sense of" as a place where conflict is inevitable, where the struggle over wages is a fact of life, where workers typically "die of boredom" and where unions provide meaningful protections against abuse. Rather, the training discourse implicitly denies that the workplace is riven with conflict and oppression. A patronizing message that working people, despite their immense experience and know-how, lack sufficient skills and experience for the new economy is hammered home. The experiences of working people who suddenly find themselves "out on the curb" due to profit-grubbing corporate layoffs are re-cast as questions about skill deficiencies in the face of the "post-industrial" economy. As Anne Gray once put it: "Class solidarity has no place in this framework."[13]

The training regime is far removed from the genuine worker education evident in Silver Donald Cameron's *The Education of Everett Richardson*, a book about the Canso fishers' strike in Nova Scotia in the early 1970s. With revealing chapter headings like "Grade School: Who Needs a Union," "High School: On Strike" and "University: Not a Contract to Write Home About," the book describes how the "country cunning" of the striking fishers helped them develop a profound insight into the conflictual dynamics at the core of the profit-making system. The Canso fishers received an education in the grandest sense of the term.[14] The training discourse in no way legitimizes the insights that Everett Richardson and his comrades formed concerning the brutal nature of the capitalist social relations. On the contrary, it figures prominently in the making of the new "de-socialized" worker required by the capitalist labour market. John Shields' commentary on job retraining programs in Canada captures some of these ideological elements: "The rhetoric of skill enhancement... stands in stark contrast to the reality of contemporary labour-market developments and conditions in which 'learn-fare,' for instance, becomes a disciplinary tool to achieve public sector fiscal restraint and a greater labour market flexibility."[15] By helping to recast the prevailing conception of working life the training regime becomes another important element in the neoliberal class struggle. As Phil Mizen wrote of youth training in Britain: "It may be 'grinding, everyday, unspectacular' class struggle, but it must be understood as class struggle all the same...."[16] The training regime, to twist Friere's famous title facetiously, is the "pedagogy of the oppressors."

As might be expected, it appears that antipathy towards unions and the labour movement has also become commonplace among elites in Canada and elsewhere. Obmundson and Doyle's study of the attitude of Canadian elites towards unions draws attention to this development. They point out that there was general sympathy with organized labour in the media, governments and the academy in the early post-war decades, sympathy that even extended to "management" on occasion, and support that was evident, for example, in an openness in the early 1980s to the establishment of tripartite decision-making structures with labour as a full partner.[17] This receptivity and sympathy, they contend, has lessoned considerably in recent years:

> Internationally, that portion of the intellectual left highly supportive of labour has been in steady decline since the late 1970s, a process that was accentuated by the collapse of the Soviet empire in 1989. Many academics formerly supportive of unions have moved on to post-materialist social issues, politically impotant post-modernism or, in the words of Carrol Ratner, undergone "prudent apostasy." The steadily increasing influence of Pope John-Paul II seems to have succeeded in moderating Catholic social criticism. The embarrassing financial scandal associated with Canada's most radical cleric, Bishop Remi de Roo, seemed almost to put an exclamation point to this decline. The advent of the right wing National Post seemed to signal similar developments in the media. Finally, a judiciary which has been activist and liberal on other issues has ruled against labour on a number of key points.[18]

Prudent apostasy aside, much of the Canadian elite, especially in the business world, has never been terribly fond of the labour movement. Michael Bliss's remarks on the attitudes of capital toward unions in the early twentieth century are always worth bearing in mind:

> The much trumpeted business 'recognition' of trade unionism before World War I reduced itself to this: workingmen have a right to form an organization to *try* to bargain with employers, to *try* to shut down a firm by going on strike. But, as the *Monetary Times* summarized the new system, 'recognition does not imply compliance with all or *any* demands which a union might make. Employers had equal rights to refuse any concessions, to fire workers who went out on strike, and to smash unions by bringing in strikebreakers. They also had a right, under the theory of individual freedom of contract, to ask workingmen voluntarily to contract away their right to join societies that would limit their individual rights.[19]

Just how far back the attitudes of the business elite in Canada have snapped is hard to establish, and, as evident in Tony Comper's remarks above, the attack on unions is more ideologically sophisticated today, but it is clear that anti-unionism is once again culturally pervasive.

As ice hockey is part of the "Canadian identity," it can be used to illustrate the spirit of the anti-unionism that pervades contemporary Canadian culture. During the lockout of 2004–2005 National Hockey League Commissioner Gary Bettman routinely referred to the National Hockey League Players' Association as the "union," a word steeped in opprobrium after decades of anti-union calumny and one that he could count on to weaken support for the players. When the lockout ended, Bettman shifted gears and accordingly spoke again of the "association," a term more commensurate with the idea that the players had capitulated by accepting a salary cap and wisely saw themselves as part of a shared journey with the NHL owners. The ease with which Bettman could shift his labels in this case shows that we "have" language just as surely as we are "had" by it, but it also shows that simple usage can lean heavily upon shifting attitudes.

These are elements in the ideological reconstruction of working life in the neoliberal era. The older notion of the Fordist worker had burned itself into social consciousness after several decades of labour struggle. It was much truer to the grinding political realities of the capitalist workplace and especially reflective of the vulnerabilities from which working people strive to protect themselves. The Fordist conception of working life could be regarded as one that ratified the historic gains of the labour movement at the level of everyday thought, confirming most fundamentally that unions are inevitable in an economy plagued with basic contradictions and that they can help to provide meaningful protections against employer abuse. In striking contrast — pun intended perhaps — the ideas associated with the neoliberal worker are culturally top-heavy. The neoliberal conception of working life has been shaped much more by the exigencies of corporate profit-making than by the organic tensions endemic to capitalist workplaces. Victor Lippit's discussion of the U.S. economy provides an indication of some of the trends and pressures that have eroded the Fordist conception of working life:

> American capitalism in 2004 differs dramatically from American capitalism in 1954.... In the 1950s powerful unions confronted powerful corporations, and collective bargaining was widely accepted.... With pensions and seniority protections, many workers felt that as long as they did their work conscientiously, they could expect to remain with the same employer through their working lives. The relations between capital and labour have changed sharply since the 1950s. Restructuring and downsizing have become routine in the modern corporation. Pressed by intense competition, both domestic and foreign, corporations are accustomed to taking a tough stance vis-à-vis their workforces. In the private sectors, the proportion of workers who are union members has declined sharply, from more than 30 percent in the 1950s to less than 10 percent today, and *most workers are well aware that loyalty, long service, and conscientiousness provide no guarantee of job security*.[20]

The following remarks by David Kotz and Martin Wolfson on the cultivation of a flexible workforce also provide an insight into the relationship between ideas about the new worker and shifting corporate ambitions:

> The cultivation of a stable workforce should be replaced with a readiness to shed large numbers of employees. As computers make inventory control and demand management more accurate, corporations say they need a more *flexible workforce*. They need to pare back to a smaller core of permanent employees and supplement their workforce with contingent and temporary employees who could be added and subtracted with ease. The workforce must adapt to this new practice, *trading a stable career in a single company for the life of an independent contractor or temporary employee*.[21]

The fields of social discourse have picked up on these changing requirements of the corporate world and loosely knitted together a revised conception of the capitalist toiler that is now "in the air." This conception glosses over the alienation and contradictory workplace experiences that are the essence of capitalist working life. The new label of "associate" promotes the idea of relatively unprotected workers whose prosperity and well-being are tied directly to beneficent employers.

The conception of the neoliberal worker forms a backdrop to contemporary life. But the degree to which working people are more likely to think of their *working-self* in neoliberal rather than Fordist terms is difficult to gauge. For example, to what degree does a poorly paid coffee-shop server see the designation "associate" as a transparent ruse? Or, to what degree is a non-unionized factory worker motivated to work extra-long hours simply because she fears for her job or needs the extra cash in the face of inadequate wages? The growth of "non-standard work," marked by irregular hours and employment, likely means that many people experience working life in a way that accords with some of the new emphasis on "flexibility." On the whole, it must be the case that these new ideas, especially the emphatic anti-union ones, complicate the workplace experience for many wage earners. It is likely that the top-heavy, neoliberal conception of working life, borne of corporate needs, has helped chisel away at the established worker by softening resistance, weakening militancy and undermining unionization drives. But the confrontational dynamics of the capitalist workplace and good, old-fashioned worker savvy probably go a long way to preventing claims about natural cooperation or an identity of interests from becoming easily lodged in the consciousness of the working class.

Labour Law in the Neoliberal Era

In early December 2008 the intricate relationship between labour law and the class struggle was thrown into relief in Weyburn, Saskatchewan. In a seventy-one-page decision and more than four years after the United Food and Commercial Workers Union applied for certification, the province's Labour Relations Board granted the request to unionize the Walmart in Weyburn. So hostile is the world's largest corporation to unions that it has been known to close down stores that become unionized. In December 2005, the Quebec Labour Relations Board, for example, found Walmart guilty of firing workers unfairly because it closed down its Jonquière store after a successful organizing drive. The mayor of Weyburn, not surprisingly, immediately expressed concern that her town of about 10,000 people might be confronted with the same fate as the residents of Jonquière. "We're very concerned about losing a major retailer in our community," Mayor Debra Button said. "We worked too hard to get the Walmart here. If the decision by Walmart is to close the store, we'll certainly be feeling that." The anxious mayor, in fact, had penned a letter to the head of Walmart in Canada to clarify the company's plans for its Weyburn outlet.[22] For its part the company expressed objection to the decision on the basis that its Weyburn "associates" had not had the opportunity to vote on the union: "We're disappointed," bemoaned Walmart spokesperson Andrew Pelletier, "clearly, you know, our associates have been denied here a vote. They've been denied a democratic process. And we believe they should have that process."[23] Pelletier added: "The fact that you've got a store now with 104 associates and only 29 of them were even there at the time of the union's application, really speaks to the fact that it would be a bit of a stretch to assume that there is widespread support at that store for this union."[24]

The notoriously anti-union company was framing its objection with an eye to attempts to organize Saskatchewan stores in North Battleford and Moose Jaw and to new provincial labour regulations that required workers to vote on a union prior to its certification. The new certification laws were part of a bundle of changes that the provincial government enacted in the spring of 2008, changes that reformed a number of elements of Saskatchewan's *Trade Union Act* in favour of business. The third amendment of this basket of reforms made representational voting necessary prior to union certification, replacing the card system, which allowed certification when a sufficient number of employees, typically at least 50 percent, had signed cards supporting the union. (This is precisely the issue that American labour is pinning its hopes on with respect to the Obama administration's *Employee Free Choice Act*, legislation that would permit the card-based certification of unions. Predictably, business interests in the U.S. are opposed to such a move, especially since the onset of the acute economic crisis in the fall of 2008.) In its grant of certification at the Weyburn Walmart, the Saskatchewan Labour Relations Board had not applied the more recent certification protocols, and the union-hating company was obviously displeased. But why did Walmart want the new vote system? Because voting is open to anti-union intervention by employers willing to strongarm its employees. The voting system favours the business community by making it more difficult to organize the workplace. Labour groups had vociferously opposed this amendment to the legislation, along with most of the other ones, arguing correctly that it would have deleterious consequences for organizing drives across the province.[25]

Walmart's reference to due democratic process reflected its support for legal changes that would help to keep unions out of its stores. Of course, the issue is not really about democracy in any way, but rather about supporting reforms that make it more difficult for workers to unionize. More to the point, capital will rhetorically support any "democratic" measure that assists its drive to accumulate, as Canadians witnessed dramatically in 1999 when Tom d'Aquino, head of Canada's leading lobby group for transnational capital, openly championed the principles of parliamentary democracy in the face of street-level protests in Seattle. The Fraser Institute, Canada's right-wing equivalent to the troubling Heritage Foundation in the United States, has recently published materials questioning the extent of union democracy, drawing particular attention to the purportedly undemocratic nature of the card-based certification process.[26] Such rhetorical strategies are part of more generalized efforts by the corporate world to reform labour laws to make it harder to unionize a workplace. As was the case in Saskatchewan in 2008, the business community has often found willing allies in conservative governments in a number of North American jurisdictions.

The discussions surrounding the unionization of employees in Weyburn shows that the class struggle is played out partially in the legal system. The neoliberal legal strategy amounts to a two-pronged effort to decrease the contingent of Fordist workers on one side and expand the ranks of the neoliberal or unprotected workers on the other. To grasp this strategy fully we must pause for a moment and reflect on the nature and development of labour law in Canada. In the not too distant past, prevailing workplace conventions and most corresponding laws of the land were wholly stacked against the wage worker. The gradual pressure that organized labour and leftish political parties brought to bear on these conventions in the early post-World War II period contributed to the development of laws that gave workers modest protections. There are two ways of seeing the historical development of progressive labour laws in Canada. With an eye to the social relations of class power in a capitalist society — the "sociological perspective" — this development reflects the inevitable struggle of working people against the excesses of employers and the owners of capital. Labour laws, from this perspective, plug into the relative balance of power between the classes, and the historical struggle was a response to the prevailing customs and laws, which were decisively on the side of the propertied class. In terms of grander matters like "fairness" or "justice" — a "metaphysically transcending standpoint" — the development of progressive labour laws reflects pressure by the working class to establish workplace standards that accord with these lofty principles. When considered together, the forward press for progressive labour laws was a positive development against the abuses of the owners of capital and in accordance with the principles of a more just and equitable society.

But labour law is Janus-faced. When we train our analysis more sensitively on the relationship between progressive labour laws and the social relations of class power in capitalist societies, it becomes evident that such laws are two-sided or contradictory. On the good side, they have been positive achievements for the working class as it struggles against the abuse of employers, and they help to lock in gains against opportunistic rollbacks. Perhaps there is no better example of this than the difficult process through which unions came to be regarded as legal entities in Canada, a long journey that included the Nova Scotia's legal ban on worker "meetings and combinations" in 1816, Sir John A. Macdonald's politically opportunistic *Trade Union Act* of 1872, which removed the cloud of criminality that had theretofore enveloped union activity, and P.C. Order 1003 in 1944, which established the lawful framework for the recognition of unions and catalyzed the post-war provincial labour relations regimes. The legal recognition of unions forced employers to regard them as a fact of economic life, which lessened the exposure of union organizers to summary reprisals and increased the confidence of workers, especially during organizing drives. The development of progressive labour laws also enshrined universal baselines of appropriate workplace conduct. These important developments gave some workers modest recourse in the event of poor treatment and put some pressure on bad-apple employers to improve wages and working conditions that fell well below industry standards. The early minimum wage laws in Canada, for example, were often designed to provide modest protections for women, who were especially vulnerable to pay-scales that fell far below the already pitiful low wages of the day. Within the context of capitalist society, labour laws empower workers and, given the scale of past injustices, they have to be regarded as historic achievements of the working class.

And yet, even progressive labour laws engender negative consequences for working people. In the early decades of Canadian capitalism the working class fought successfully to bring workplaces under a regulatory framework, but these regulations came with steep trade-offs and political costs. The following examples give a sense of these sacrifices or lost opportunities:

- Although labour standards seemingly provide worker protections, the benchmarks are set so as not to offend the leading non-unionized industries of the day.
- Labour codes create the sense of universal standards, which draws attention away from the generally much better standards in unionized facilities.[27]
- The state appears to be a neutral guarantor of worker rights when in fact it is merely ratifying prevailing low-end conventions.
- Labour legislation has always been crafted to protect the general accumulation interests of capital first and foremost, even the post-war labour relations laws that helped to smooth out production.
- Many laws were specifically enacted to forestall or co-opt mounting working-class protests.
- The enactment of much labour relations law in Canada was tacitly associated with the repudiation of the radical left by organized labour, including the purging of its ranks.
- The establishment of the progressive legal regime coincided with labour's historical acquiescence on the question of managerial prerogative over the labour process.

45

- The apparatus of the legal regime is mostly "over and above" working people, who accordingly lose the invaluable capacity to challenge and alter shopfloor or office practices directly.
- The rhythms of the legal regime were an important element in the bureaucratization of unions and their relative de-politicization.

The historic development of progressive labour laws in Canada undoubtedly contributed to the equally historic declawing of the labour movement in the post-World War II era. And, as witnessed in recent decades, all the labour laws in the world provide little protection against mass layoffs, industrial restructuring, deteriorating wages and the generalized class war on working people.

Two specific aspects of these political costs warrant further attention, one pertaining to the essential nature of the legal regime and the second to working-class consciousness. The implicit structure of the legal regime militates against the strengthening of working-class politics. Most of this effect spins out the Manichean nature of the regime, i.e., its propensity to regard everything as either *legal* or *illegal*. As workplaces became highly regulated sites of production, employers, organized labour and non-unionized workers alike had to function within the legal parameters or face penalties. The grievance procedure became the dominant process to establish transgressions. Working-class capacity to resist narrowed measurably by virtue of the circumscription of options. Most of the gritty strategies of working-class struggle, ranging from factory occupations to sympathy strikes, became illegal. Julie Guard's thoughtful reflections on the Supreme Court ruling of 2007 that defined collective bargaining as a fundamental right provide helpful examples of the difficult relationship between the law and the social relations of class.[28] In speaking specifically of the advent of legal unions, she writes:

> Having acquired the approval of the political establishment, unions became part of the mainstream. Legally certified unions were entitled to an array of rights, including the right to strike and to bargain with employers on behalf of their members. But their right to strike was severely restricted. Under the terms of the compromise, unions could no longer engage in mid-contract strikes and sympathy strikes. Yet this kind of rank-and-file militancy was precisely what had prompted the legislation that now constrained them. Public sector workers used illegal strikes in the 1960s in a similar manner to win legal rights, specifically, the right to bargain collectively and, in some provinces, the right to strike. But this exception proves the rule. Except in unusual, indeed, historically significant, circumstances, industrial conflict was strictly contained

and, aside from strikes supporting contract bargaining, channelled into bureaucratic processes.[29]

And with respect to the containment of union members by unions she adds:

> Unions, not management, were responsible for maintaining a disciplined workforce that adhered to the provisions bargained in the contract. This effectively required them to police their own members. Members prone to shop floor agitation were no longer an asset to the union; they became a liability. Rank-and-file activism had to be firmly controlled, and unions began to see rank-and-file participation as more trouble than it was worth. Rank-and-file activists were amateurs, and increasingly, union work required experts. Administering collective agreements, processing grievances and bargaining became too complicated for the ordinary member who lack specialized skills. Over time, unions acquired a layer of professional staff who provided high-quality services to members but further separated them from the activity of the union.[30]

In the end, even a legal regime with progressive labour laws means that political spontaneity is tamed, gestures of solidarity are impaired and the class struggle is generally blunted. "Where there is power," it might be said, borrowing misleadingly from Foucault's famous expression, "there can only be *legal* resistance."

The legal regime also militates against the elevation of working-class consciousness. In writing of the effects of contractual strikes and the loss of the option of sympathy strikes with the consolidation of the new post-World War II labour regime, Craig Heron writes: "It is doubtful that any other legislation constrained class consciousness as effectively among Canadian workers over the next fifty years."[31] This effect can be summarized in terms of the paradox that the enactment of progressive labour laws reflects a rise in working-class consciousness, a rise that is then eroded by virtue of those laws themselves. It is, perhaps, one of the greatest ironies of life in capitalist society that oppressive labour laws probably do more for the development of working-class consciousness than progressive ones. The principle mechanism at work here is the manner in which labour laws construe economic conflict. The legal regime tends to regard workers and workplaces as discrete entities, as individuals or organizations with economic protections and rights. Working people learn to gaze *inward* upon their own workplaces rather than *outward* at other workers in the economy. A worker, for example, grieving against workplace infractions is never quite the same thing, politically speaking, as a wage labourer standing shoulder to shoulder with fellow workers against industry-wide abuse or society-wide mistreatment. These individuated procedures follow their way through the legal regime's administrative array of boards, tribunals and courts. The working class as a whole can never grieve, nor can it be a plaintiff. Working people, in addition to being hemmed in by labour laws and a legal regime that delineates permissible practices as legal or illegal, are encouraged to think of themselves as individuals with specified economic privileges or entitlements. The legal regime essentially dis-aggregates the working class and promotes subtle ideas about an *economy* populated by *productive citizens*. By virtue of the legal regime the citizen-worker is anointed with a virtuous civic-mindedness in the economic sphere just as the citizen-voter, owing to the electoral process, is so anointed in the political sphere. Class struggle is fractionated and becomes a highly suffused affair at the point of production, and class politics accordingly withers, to the great benefit of the capitalist class. In considering this manner in which the legal regime militates against working-class consciousness and the collective sense of shared struggle, it might be said that "class power does not come from below," to modify another of Foucault's famous observations about power, "but is rather stationed in the legal regime that promotes a wholly liberal (or individuated) way of framing economic struggle."

It is important to stress that the legal regime attenuated working-class politics in the post-World War II decades,[32] and this effect has been intensified in the neoliberal era. The law has become another weapon in the disciplinary arsenal of the capitalist class. Lawful changes have targeted all workers, irrespective of the character of their employment, and given rise to political pressure to expand and deepen the regulatory frameworks that govern the workplace. For established workers, the laws are designed to minimize the overall impact of unions, especially through strikes, and to lower the overall rate of unionization in society. And for unprotected workers — often called "non-standard" workers because of their irregular employment and irregular hours of work, or "precarious" workers because of their susceptibility to low wages, poor working conditions and unhealthy working arrangements — the laws are broadly designed to keep them in their place. It is a pincer movement at the legal level that targets both spheres of the segmented labour market simultaneously: an attack on the established worker is complemented by legal strategies designed to perpetuate the condition of the more rapidly expanding segment of unprotected workers.

Sometimes these neoliberal effects are obscured, especially when labour scores a rare legal victory, as when sympathetic governments pass progressive legal reforms or when the courts rule in their favour. In November 2008, for example, the Ontario Court of Appeal ruled that the province's *Agricultural Employees Protection Act*, prohibiting the unionization of farm workers, violated the right to freedom of association enshrined in the Canadian Charter of Rights and Freedoms. Recent decades have occasionally seen statutory flip-flops as progressive governments change laws in a more pro-labour direction and conservative governments make them more friendly to capital. The Saskatchewan government and business interests, for example, defended the 2008 reforms as redressing a long-standing imbalance in provincial labour laws that had favoured labour since the *Trade Union Act* of the CCF (Co-operative Commonwealth Federation) government in 1944 and that had been worsened by successive pro-labour governments. In the early 2000s the New Democratic government in Manitoba redressed some of the legal rollbacks enacted by Conservative governments in the 1990s. In Ontario in the early 1990s, the NDP government enacted labour reforms that included anti-scab legislation; these laws were immediately rolled back by the Conservative government upon its election in the mid-1990s. Despite this see-sawing back and forth, on the whole neoliberalism has weakened progressive labour laws and availed itself fully of the ethos of legalism that paralyzes working-class politics. Although an exhaustive review of changes in labour laws across the country are beyond the scope of this book, the following general observations characterize the process during the neoliberal era.

Legal Militancy against Organized Labour

Laws that empower working people collectively have tended to be weakened. This strategy is most obvious in the restrictions placed on unions. Since no government can now declare unions to be illegal without appearing archaic, the strategy has shifted to using the law to make it more difficult to form unions. There is evidence that certifications in jurisdictions like Ontario are down in the wake of provincial legal reforms similar to the 2008 anti-union laws in Saskatchewan.[33] Most provinces do not have anti-scab legislation, which assists workers during strikes, and the anti-labour climate is so hostile that a minority parliament in Ottawa could put the issue of "replacement workers" to bed publicly in 2007 with the defeat of Bill C-257, and do so without any apparent political ramifications. Governments routinely cut down public sector strikes and have tended to widen the definition of "essential services," thereby continuing the "assault on trade union freedoms."[34]

Deregulation

Some areas of the law have simply been deregulated, with one strategy being to widen the field of statutory exemptions. Reforms to labour law in British Columbia, for example, expanded the definitions of "farmwork," "long-haul truck driver," "high technology professional" and "manager," designations that were exempted from many employment standards regulations.[35] The deregulation of child labour in British Columbia, which now permits children to work as much as adults in some situations and which risks exposing them to dangerous circumstances, has garnered critical attention.[36] In 2005, the

Alberta government, to cite another case that shows how labour laws are relaxed to respond to the needs of industries clamouring for cheap labour, removed the requirement that forced children aged twelve to fourteen to receive government approval before commencing work in the food services industry. The relaxation of labour codes was evident when changes in Ontario's *Employment Standards Act* in 2000 raised the possible number of weekly hours of work and permitted the averaging of overtime hours.[37] The scaling back of regulations continues to be a carefully construed strategy to bring the law in line with the leading low-standard industries of the day, one of the oldest themes in the historical development of Canadian labour law.[38]

Administrative Atrophy

Laws amount to very little when compliance is low. In many jurisdictions around the world some of the best labour laws are rendered ineffective by weak enforcement. As in many other fields of governmental oversight and monitoring in the neoliberal era, staff reductions have hollowed labour law enforcement. Specific strategies include a reduction in the number of field inspectors, limiting investigative discretion of inspectors, the rationalization and closure of field offices and the weakening of mechanisms through which complaints are reported.[39]

Narrow Regulatory Scope

In some areas of employment the state has sluggishly failed to widen the scope of labour protections. This is evident in the case of those employees dubiously classified as "self-employed," workers who nevertheless only have their labour power to sell.[40] It is also evident in the more general area of "non-standard" (sometimes also called atypical, precarious and contingent work), which includes part-time employees, "temp" workers, casual workers, migrant workers and seasonal workers. These rapidly expanding areas of employment fall outside the "standard" job typified by a set number of regular hours week after week. The low level of regulation of these types of employment fails to address many of the key vulnerabilities routinely faced by these workers, who are more often than not women and persons of colour.[41]

Moral Suasion

Neoliberal governments have used legal regulations to drive home the message of austerity and restraint. Although examples abound, like an unwillingness of provincial governments to move on the issue of "pay equity," the outstanding example of this inclination is the failure to peg minimum wage levels to inflation (discussed extensively in chapter 4). This failure has resulted in the minimum wage losing measurable buying-power over the last three decades and has helped governments play a leading role in wage restraint throughout the economy. In the area of interest rates, economists call this "moral suasion." In this sense the wage signal of neoliberal governments is akin to the Bank of Canada's role when it establishes its trend-setting interest rate.

Rhetorical Disingenuousness

Many reforms are justified using the alluring rhetoric of "flexibility," which acts as a cover for the real intent of the changes. Commenting on the B.C. government's discussion paper entitled *Fair and Effective: A Review of Employment Standards in British Columbia*, the provincial federation of labour offered a politically astute assessment: "The term workplace flexibility is often used to obscure what is really happening to workers. Flexibility is about downgrading or deregulating basic protections. While business lobby groups would have us believe otherwise, the push for greater 'flexibility' will simply shift more costs on to workers."[42] Seth Klein's observations on the same provincial initiatives were equally pointed: "At the core of the proposed changes is a demand from powerful business lobby groups for increased workplace 'flexibility' — a euphemism for workers more willing to work for less pay and/or accept inferior work conditions."[43]

Conclusion

Much of neoliberalism is about rendering workers sufficiently pliant to be delivered into the hands of the labour market without "attitude." The goal is to herd the working class into jobs characterized by lower pay, irregular hours and poor working conditions. The evolving regulatory regime in Canada has helped to insure this outcome. It has helped guarantee that the pool of vulnerable workers expands relative to the pool of established or Fordist workers. It thereby directly promotes the idea that unionized industrial workers with decent wages, secure jobs and meaningful protections are a relic of the past, unsuited to the realities of the new "post-capitalist" economy.

The shifting conceptions of work and the neoliberal legal assault are two aspects of the generalized attack on working people. These efforts to weaken the overall power of the working-class aim to lower wages and restore rates of profitability. In the next chapter two other manifestations of this attack are explored: the declining rates of unionization and the declining levels of militancy on the part of organized labour. It concludes by demonstrating that neoliberalism has achieved its goal and that the trend of rising real wages that characterized the Fordist era in Canada was arrested by the late 1970s. The neoliberal agenda has been remarkably successful — and remarkably devastating.

Notes

1. "Workers May Have Reasons to Cheer in 2007," *Globe and Mail*, December 27, 2006, Section B, p. 12. Information and website taken from article.

2. Bruce Campbell, *20 Years Later: Has Free Trade Delivered on its Promise?* Canadian Centre for Policy Alternatives, North American Deep Integration Series, 1: 2 (December 2007), p. 5.

3. See Tony Fang and Anil Verma, "Union Wage Premium," *Perspectives on Labour and Income* 4: 4 (Winter 2002).

4. Jeffrey Harrod, *Power, Production and the Unprotected Worker* (New York, NY: Columbia University Press, 1987), pp. 39–40.

5. Organisation for Economic Co-operation and Development, *Growing Unequal? Income Distribution and Poverty in OECD Countries*, October 2008, p. 25–26.

6. The article by Thomas Piketty and Emmanuel Saez entitled "Income Inequality in the United States, 1913–1998," *The Quarterly Journal of Economics* 118: 1 (February 2003), pp. 1–39, shows how income distribution was altered, but it also shows that there was nothing approaching an equitable distribution of income in the post-war era.

7. This is the line taken in the more recent writings of David Harvey, *A Brief History of Neoliberalism* (Oxford University Press, 2005), and in Gérard Duménil and Dominique Lévy, "Neoliberal Income Trends: Wealth, Class and Ownership in the USA," *New Left Review* 30 (November/December 2004), pp. 105–133. Conceptualizing class in terms of income levels rather than in relation to productive life runs risks that are probably not worth the analytical trouble and certainly not very helpful politically.

8. James W. Rinehart, *The Tyranny of Work: Alienation and the Labour Process*, 5th ed. (Toronto: Thomson Nelson, 2006), p. 71.

9. Tony Comper, "The End of Hierarchy," Canadian Council of Chief Executives, *National and Global Perspectives*, (Summer 2005), p. 21, my emphasis.

10. Comper, my emphasis.

11. Many of these points are elaborated in Thom Workman and David Bedford, *Worker-Centred Training in an Economy-Centred World: The Challenge for Labour*, Centre for Research on Work and Society (2000–3), pp. 1–12.

12. Manfred Bienefeld, "Capitalism and the Nation State in the Dog Days of the Twentieth Century," *Socialist Register* (London: The Merlin Press, 1994), pp. 113–14.

13. Anne Gray, "New Labour — New Labour Discipline," *Capital and Class* 65 (Summer 1998), p. 2.

14. Silver Donald Cameron, *The Education of Everett Richardson: The Nova Scotia Fishermen's Strike 1970–71* (Toronto: McClelland and Stewart Limited, 1977).

15. John Shields, "Flexible Work, Labour Market Polarization, and the Politics of Skill Training and Enhancement," in *The Training Trap: Ideology, Training and the Labour Market*, Dunk et al., eds. (Halifax: Fernwood, 1996).

16. See Phil Mizen's general discussion in "In and Against the Training State," *Capital and Class* 53 (Summer 1994), pp. 99–121, quote from p. 114.

17. See R. Ogmundson and M. Doyle, "The Rise and Decline of Canadian Labour, 1960 to 2000: Elites, Power, Ethnicity and Gender," *Canadian Journal of Sociology* 27: 3 (2002), discussion on pp. 422–25.

18. Ogmundson and Doyle, pp. 425–26.

19. Michael Bliss, *A Living Profit: Studies in the Social History of Canadian Business, 1883–1911* (Toronto: McClelland and Stewart, 1974), p. 87.

20. Victor D. Lippit, "Class Struggles and the Reinvention of American Capitalism in

the Second Half of the Twentieth Century," *Review of Radical Political Economics* 36: 3 (Summer 2004), p. 336, my emphasis.

21. David M. Kotz and Martin H. Wolfson, "Déjà Vu All Over Again: The 'New' Economy in Historical Perspective," *Labor Studies Journal*, 28: 4 (Winter 2004), p. 27, my emphasis.

22. "Saskatchewan Mayor Worried Walmart Will Close Unionized Store," *Canadian Broadcasting Corporation* <http://www.cbc.ca/consumer/story/2008/12/10/[-] wal-mart-weyburn.html> last accessed December 9, 2008.

23. "Union Certified at Walmart Store in Saskatchewan," *Canadian Broadcasting Corporation* <http://www.cbc.ca/canada/saskatchewan/story/2008/12/09/wal-mart.html> last accessed December 9, 2008.

24. "Union Certified at Walmart Store in Saskatchewan."

25. See discussion in Jim Warren, *Joining the Race to the Bottom: An Assessment of Bill 6, Amendments to the Trade Union Act, 2008,* Canadian Centre for Policy Alternatives (Saskatchewan Office, March 2008).

26. An example of this ideological struggle can be seen in Jason Clemens and Keith Godin, "The 'Un-democracy' of Unions: Advocacy for Automatic Certification and Lack of Disclosure Requirements Undermine Credibility," *Fraser Forum* (February, 2008). Not surprisingly for an institution funded for the sole purpose of reaching corporate-friendly conclusions, the authors, after setting out a remarkably limited set of criteria for the measure of democracy and utterly oblivious to the social relations of power and intimidation that surround the workplace, conclude that unions are undemocratic: "The challenge for union leaders," they write in a way that would gladden the hearts of the Institute's corporate bankrollers, "is to start living by their own words and principles," p. 29.

27. Mark Thomas's discussion of Ontario's post-war regulatory codes provides one of the better discussions on the relatively weaker protections of the non-unionized segments of the labour market. See "Setting the Minimum: Ontario's Employment Standards in the Postwar Years, 1944–1968," *Labour/Le Travail* 54 (Fall 2004).

28. Julie Guard, "How Important are Labour-Friendly Laws to Manitoba's Unions?" Canadian Centre for Policy Alternatives Review, *Labour Notes,* July 2008. Guard's brief analysis of this decision is sound: "But important though this court decision is, legal decisions like this one will not make the labour movement stronger. The dynamic works the other way. Good labour laws don't make strong unions; strong unions make for better labour laws." Unpaginated, para. 3.

29. Guard, para. 9.

30. Guard, para. 10.

31. Craig Heron, *The Canadian Labour Movement: A Short History*, 2nd edition (Toronto: James Lorimer, 1996), p. 79.

32. For a creative and thoughtful proposal to break this stultifying trend see Bryan D. Palmer, "What's Law Got to Do With It? Historical Considerations on Class Struggle, Boundaries of Constraint, and Capitalist Authority," *Osgoode Hall Law Journal* 41: 2 & 2 (2003), pp. 465–90.

33. Sara Slinn, "The Effect of Compulsory Certification Votes on Certification Applications in Ontario: An Empirical Analysis," *Canadian Labour and Employment Law Journal,* 10: 3 (2003), pp. 399–429.

34. An excellent survey of these trends can be found in Leo Panitch and Donald Swartz, *From Consent to Coercion: The Assault on Trade Union Freedoms,* 3rd ed., (Toronto: Garamond, 2003).

35. See the excellent discussion in David Fairey, *Eroding Worker Protections: British Columbia's New "Flexible" Employment Standards,* Canadian Centre for Policy Alternatives (November 2005), pp. 17–19, p. 25 and elsewhere.

36. See Helesia Luke and Graeme Moore, *Who's Looking Out for Our Kids? Deregulating Child Labour Law in British Columbia,* Canadian Centre for Policy Alternatives (British Columbia Office, March 2004). The authors astutely assess the basic impetus to these changes when they write: "Bill 37 transforms the significance of child employment in the economy. Child employment is moving from an opportunity to learn or earn pocket money to becoming a source of cheap labour for low-skilled employment," p. 22.

37. An excellent critique of the changes in Ontario may be found in Judy Fudge, "Flexibility and Feminization: The New Ontario Employment Standards Act," *Journal of Law and Social Policy* 16 (2001), pp. 1–22.

38. See discussion in Fairey, *Eroding Worker Protections* p. 20, where the minimum daily shift, for example, was reduced from four hours to two hours to accommodate the service sector, especially in retail and food industries. Also see the attentive discussion in Warren, *Joining the Race,* where it appears that pressure for Saskatchewan's reforms were coming partially from the retail sector in need of low-skilled, low-paid employees, p. 14.

39. The B.C. case provides another excellent example of this disturbing practice. See Fairey, *Eroding Worker Protections,* note 36.

40. See the excellent article by Judy Fudge entitled "Labour Protection for Self-employed Workers," *Just Labour,* 3 (Fall 2003). Fudge concludes: "It is time to revise the basis for determining the scope of application of labour, social wage, and tax legislation." As for part-time workers she writes: "All workers who depend on the sale of their capacity to work should be covered by labour protection and social insurance legislation…" quotes from p. 43 and p. 44 respectively.

41. On the non-regulation of precarious work under the NAFTA framework see Leah F. Vosko, "Regulating Preciousness?: The Temporary Employment Relationship under the NAFTA and the EC Treaty," *Relations industrielles* 53: 1 (1998), pp. 123–53. The comparisons to the more regulating European context are revealing.

42. British Columbia Federation of Labour, *Employment Standards Review Discussion Paper,* December 2001, pp. 3–4.

43. Seth Klein, *No Evidence to Justify Lowering the Floor: A Submission to the BC Employment Standards Review,* British Columbia, Canadian Centre for Policy Alternatives, January 2002, unpaginated.

3

Unionization Rate, Work Stoppages and Declining Wages

Neoliberalism has chosen no single path to the demise of the established worker. As the crisis of the auto industry in North America deepened in 2009, the rapidity with which politicians tore into the already-battered auto-workers, demanding further concessions, and, sadly, the rapidity with which the auto workers on both sides of the border expressed a willingness to make those concessions, seemed to encapsulate this historic assault on the established worker. This rollback is bound to endure long after neoliberalism has rhetorically passed. This chapter examines three other manifestations of this eclipse of the established worker: the declining rates of unionization, the falling incidence of strikes and the stagnation in real wages that began in the late 1970s.

Decline in Unionization Rates

In the first few decades of the post-1850 capitalist era, the number of unionized workers tended to undulate in step with the ups and downs of the economy. When the economy was doing well, a rise in the number of unionized workers was usually evident, even when the legal status of unions was ambiguous. When the economy slipped into a depression, the number of unionized workers would tend to fall off appreciably. As the twentieth century gathered momentum, however, there was a discernable rise in the number of workers belonging to unions, and this rise was no longer significantly influenced by the business cycle. In Canada in 1911, just 133,000 workers belonged to unions. By 1921, this figure had snaked its way up to 313,000 workers and would hover around this mark for the next fifteen years, despite the economic downturn in the early 1920s. By the late 1930s, the number of unionized workers started to rise steeply. At the termination of World War II, over 700,000 workers were unionized, and by the end of the decade, abetted by the spirit of P.C. Order 1003 and the post-war industrial relations regimes in the provinces, more than one million workers were unionized. Throughout the Fordist era the number of unionized workers rose fairly steadily and reached more than two million by 1968.[1]

As might be anticipated, the rate of unionized workers, or the number of unionized workers expressed as a percentage of the overall number of non-agricultural workers in the economy, also rose throughout the middle decades of the twentieth century. Just after World War I the unionization rate was around 15 percent. It fell for much of the 1920s but began to climb again towards the close of the decade. During the Great Depression union density continued to hover in the 15 percent range. During World War II, with the arrival of modest job security, the rate of unionization began its historic rise, and this trend continued until the early 1950s, when it settled in the range of 30 percent. As evident in chart 3.1, the rate of unionization went down slightly in the late 1950s and early 1960s, but between 1965 and 1975 it again worked its way up to stand at more than 35 percent. Between the end of World War II and the mid-1970s the overall rate of unionization rose by 20 percent.

As the Fordist compact began to unravel in the 1970s, the upward trend in the rate of unionization, and especially the noticeable rise between the mid-1960s and the mid-1970s, was brought to a halt. By the mid-1970s, the rate of unionization hovered just under 35 percent; roughly one in every three workers belonged to a union. Thereafter, as chart 3.1 displays, any growth in the number of unionized workers stayed in proportion to the overall growth in the number of working people in the Canadian economy. One of the signature protections of the Fordist worker was the acceptance of trade unions. The post-war industrial relations paradigm inevitably encouraged

Chart 3.1 Twentieth-Century Rise in Rate of Unionization, Canada, 1921–1980

Source: Data from 1921 to 1960 compiled from *Labour Organizations in Canada: 1960* (Ottawa: Department of Labour, Canada, Economics and Research Branch), p. xi; data for 1965, 1970 and 1975 complied from *Canada YearBook*, 1966, 1970–71 and 1976–77 respectively (Ottawa: Minister of Industry, Trade and Commerce, Dominion Bureau of Statistics, sub-section "Labour: Organized Labour").

union growth, although never with the enthusiasm of the *Wagner Act* south of the border. But within three decades the general rise in union density had levelled off noticeably.

Since the early 1980s, the overall rate of unionization has declined, and this decline is especially pronounced in certain sectors of the economy. As chart 3.2 shows, the overall rate of unionization declined considerably, from 37.6 percent in 1981 to 30.7 percent in 1998, with the bulk of the drop occurring between 1989 and 1998. In fact, over that decade the rate of unionization fell almost 5 percent. Sectoral declines were also significant. Manufacturing trended down from 43.9 percent to 42.2 percent between 1981 and 1989, and then fell sharply to 31.3 percent by 1998. In the construction sector, the decline of 6.6 percent during the 1980s was roughly equalled by a further decline of 6.3 percent during the 1990s. And in the troubled forestry and mining sector, a dramatic decline of 13.5 percent during the 1980s was exacerbated by an additional decline of 6.2 percent during the 1990s.

The story of declining unionization is equally dramatic at the provincial level. The most sobering tale of table 3.1 is that the overall rates of union density, along with commercial (non-public sector) rates, declined in every province between 1981 and 2004. At 11.0 percent, New Brunswick experienced the steepest overall decline in the rate of unionization. The declines in Alberta and British Columbia followed closely at 10.3 percent. Five other provinces had declines in the rate of unionization of more than 6.0 percent during the period under review. The lowest overall declines, of 2.5 percent and 2.6 percent, were in Manitoba and Saskatchewan. As a rule, the bulk of

Chart 3.2 Decline in Rate of Unionization, Canada, 1981–1998

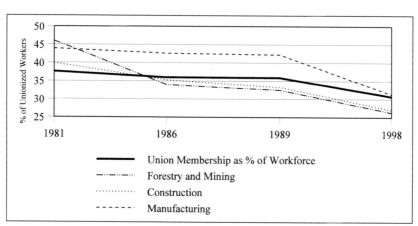

Source: Extracted and compiled from Statistics Canada, Morisette et al., "Diverging Trends in Unionization," Perspectives on Labour and Income 6: 4 (April 2005), Table 1, pp. 5–6.

these declines occurred during the 1990s, although some downward trends continued throughout the 1981 to 2004 period. In Ontario, for example, 4.8 percent of the overall decline of 6.4 percent occurred between 1989 and 1998, and the province underwent a further drop of 0.7 percent between 1998 and 2004.

Across the country the union density among public sector workers has been fairly constant throughout the neoliberal era. It is in the commercial sector where the decline has been concentrated, a trend especially evident in some provinces more than others. The steepest decline in the commercial rate of unionization occurred in British Columbia, where the rate of 36.4 percent in 1981 fell to just 21.9 percent by 2004, a stunning drop of 14.5 percent. Three Atlantic provinces, Newfoundland, Nova Scotia and New Brunswick, also experienced declines in the commercial sector of more than

Table 3.1: Declining Unionization Rates, Canada, 1981–2004

Province	Union Density	1981	1986	1989	1998	2004	Change
Newfoundland	Overall Rate	45.2	46.5	41.7	39.7	39.1	-6.1
	Commercial Rate	37.4	31.5	30.5	24.1	25.9	-11.4
P.E.I.	Overall Rate	38	29.2	31.6	26.3	30.1	-7.9
	Commercial Rate	22.5	14.6	16.7	9.9	12.8	-9.7
N.S.	Overall Rate	33.8	31.9	34.2	28.9	27.4	-6.4
	Commercial Rate	23.7	21.7	24.2	16.1	12.6	-11.1
N.B	Overall Rate	39.8	34.3	35.4	26.6	28.8	-11.0
	Commercial Rate	29.4	22.5	24.2	13.9	15.6	-13.7
Quebec	Overall Rate	44.2	43	40.8	35.7	37.4	-6.8
	Commercial Rate	34.7	32.7	32.1	23.8	26.5	-8.3
Ontario	Overall Rate	33.7	32.6	32.8	28.0	27.3	-6.4
	Commercial Rate	27.9	25.9	24.9	19.6	18.0	-9.9
Manitoba	Overall Rate	37.9	36.0	37.9	34.9	35.4	-2.5
	Commercial Rate	28.8	24.5	26.4	22.4	22.1	-6.7
Saskatchewan	Overall Rate	37.9	34.9	36.8	33.6	35.2	-2.6
	Commercial Rate	26.3	21.5	24.4	19.3	20.8	-5.5
Alberta	Overall Rate	28.4	28.5	30.1	23	33.1	-10.3
	Commercial Rate	19.8	16.0	18.3	13.3	12.2	-7.6
B.C.	Overall Rate	43.3	40.2	39.1	34.8	33.1	-10.3
	Commercial Rate	36.4	32.3	30.7	23.8	21.9	-14.5

Note: Commercial refers to non-public sector workers.
Source: Compiled from Statistics Canada, Morissette et al., "Diverging Trends in Unionization," *Perspectives on Labour and Income* 6: 4 (April 2005), Table 2, p. 7.

Chart 3.3 Sectoral Stratification in Union Coverage, Canada, 2007

Union Coverage in the Public Sector

- The rate of union coverage — workers belonging to a union or covered by a union contract — in the public sector is relatively high and has been stable since 1997.

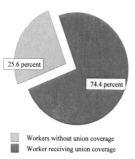

- Roughly 2.5 million of the more than 3.2 million workers in the public sector are covered by a union.

- In the neoliberal era governments have set an anti-union tone. Public sector unions have been weakened by such devices as expanding the notion of "essential service," by resorting to back-to-work legislation, government downsizing, public-private partnerships and contracting out. The fact that unionization rates have not increased likely points to the partial success of this strategy.

25.6 percent

74.4 percent

■ Workers without union coverage
■ Worker receiving union coverage

Union Coverage in the Private Sector

- This concerted attack on public sector unions by successive neoliberal governments has sent a chilling signal to all workers, especially those in the private sector.

- Unionization in the private sector is only 18.6 percent.

- The frigid anti-union climate produced by neoliberal governments combined with the restructuring of capital, especially evident in the number of plant closures and relocations, has helped nudge this figure down from 21.3 percent in 1997.

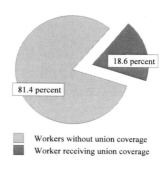

18.6 percent

81.4 percent

■ Workers without union coverage
■ Worker receiving union coverage

Accommodation and Food Service Union Coverage

- Among service workers in accommodation and food services just 8.1 percent of the workforce is covered by a union contract, down from 8.6 percent a decade earlier.

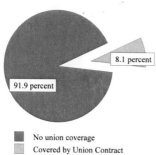

8.1 percent

91.9 percent

- Despite organizational drives in recent years by unions like the UFCW or UNITE-HERE, fewer than 1 in every 10 workers in this sector presently receives the modest protections afforded by a union contract.

- Anti-union ferocity in those sectors of the economy with low rates of unionization, especially fast food and retail sectors, has been well documented.

■ No union coverage
■ Covered by Union Contract

Source: Data compiled from CANSIM, Table 282-0077.

10.0 percent during this period. Ontario's commercial sector decline of 9.9 percent is also noteworthy, followed closely by the decline in Prince Edward Island of 9.7 percent. No province experienced a decline in the commercial rate of unionization of less than 5.0 percent.

The decline in union density in Canada is not as quite as severe as the 15 percent or more decline in the United States. A growing body of literature has advanced a wide range of explanations for the decrease, ranging from the natural evolution of capitalist societies away from their inherently conflictual tendencies to the rise of globalization.[2] Researchers sensitive to the social relations of class power in the neoliberal era have proffered the following explanations for the decline in union density:

- the weakening of traditional unionized economic sectors, especially the manufacturing sector, with its intensive global-wide restructuring, and the resource sector, riven with plant rationalizations and closures;
- the chilly anti-union climate, fuelled by the cultural ideas about the new worker and the new economy, and supported by the idea that unions are antiquated;[3]
- neoliberal policies, including privatization, government downsizing and contracting out;
- the expansion of employment in firms without unions and in sectors of the economy where unions are uncommon, including the clerical, informational, agricultural and retail sectors;
- laws making it harder to form unions and laws prohibiting unions from striking;
- the hostility towards unions oozing from many corporations in the service sector, including the infamous attention-grabbing anti-unionism of Walmart;
- the failure of unions to pump sufficient resources into unionization drives; and
- injurious union practices like "raiding."

The trend of the neoliberal era is clear: the historical rise in the rate of unionization has been arrested, and measurable declines are evident in recent decades.

The Eclipse of Militancy

Workers have always tended to resist capital. In the face of the monotony that typifies the alienating workplace working people will daydream, kibitz, nap, flirt, enter sports pools and partake in distractions such as music and computer games.[4] In response to the unpleasantness of work many employees will simply avoid work altogether by "calling in sick."[5] These activities form part of the fabric of the working day and help workers endure the sheer tedium of mind-numbing work. Terms like "slammin" (cheating or deceiving the employer) and "scammin" (avoiding work by lingering and loitering) are bandied around many workplaces.[6] Much of the resistance has a sort of light-hearted, almost humourous quality to it. Call centre workers have been known to carry on full-blown conversations with answering machines, hotel workers sometimes refuse to smile, auto workers have occasionally disrupted the flow of the assembly line by "dropping" a wrench into the works, bartenders have occasionally added an extra shot or two to drinks and workers in the banking sector might "fiddle" with financial sheets.[7] These strategies often share the common feature of standing firm against managerial prerogatives to control the work process for the sake of increasing productivity. Resistance in the face of perceived workplace injustices can also take on a much more aggressive character. In response to the litany of injurious decisions made by capital, workers have been known to smash machines, occupy factories, destroy or contaminate products and pour into the streets to protest. At other times they may simply abscond with some of the raw materials or the finished product, especially if they feel exploited by their employer.[8]

And then there are strikes — those moments when the resistance of working people becomes a highly collective and determined affair. A strike is infused with the spirit of worker solidarity; it centres around demands that reveal the pressing issues between labour and employers; the demands themselves are forged through experience and tend to emerge after prolonged consultation and reflection on both sides; it is a strategy likely to be deployed only when other efforts to reach a compromise have failed; and it raises the stakes in a way suggestive of a zero sum outcome. Strikes disclose the more generalized class contradictions of capitalist society. The rise of strikes in the latter part of the nineteenth century signalled the maturation of Canada as a capitalist society, especially in the period of the 1880s known as the "Great Upheaval."[9] Two earlier periods of strikes were so intense that the ruling elites responded in part by convening royal commissions to diffuse rising tensions. Why? Because strikes reveal the ultimate weakness of capital, namely, its inability to accumulate profits when workers withhold their labour power. Therewith vanishes the capitalist's *raison d'être*, the motive force that transforms a wealthy hoarder or lender of money into a capitalist producing commodities. Strikes, especially those in the manufacturing, resource, energy, transportation and communication sectors, provide a glimpse of the latent power of the working class, a power that someday, perhaps, will chase the private appropriators of socialized production from their gilded offices. Even in Canada, where this capacity of working people has yet to be realized, it is noteworthy that some strikes helped to define the political character of class relations long after they ended.[10] The Winnipeg General Strike of 1919 revealed the political ambiguity of the Canadian left in the early post-World War I period and confirmed to everyone the extent to which local business and the federal state would employ coercive measures (arrests, widespread deportations, firings and military deployment) to keep the country "peaceful," meaning free from insurrection and revolution.[11] An arbitration ruling by Supreme Court Justice Ivan C. Rand in the aftermath of the Ford Windsor strike of 1945 established what came to be known as the "Rand Formula," whereby all workers at a workplace would be required to pay union dues irrespective of their union status. At the time this was seen to be a momentous victory for organized labour.[12] Strikes sometimes have a lingering effect on class relations in intangible ways. The Dare (cookie) strike in Kitchener in the 1970s and the Irving Oil strike in Saint John in the 1990s signalled the willingness of capital to crush the spirit of the working class, just as the 2001 success of defiant Nova Scotia healthcare workers — who forced the provincial government to back down after resigning *en masse* in the wake of back-to-work legislation — counteracted much of the gloom that has beset the left in recent decades. Strikes matter!

A review of the incidence of work stoppages (mainly strikes)[13] over the twentieth century reveals distinct trends (see chart 3.4). In the early part of the century the incidence of strikes undulated sharply. A wave of strikes that hit in the aftermath of World War I was followed by an equally sharp decline in strikes during the 1920s and a return of the pattern of sharp undulations in the 1930s. With the onset of World War II an upward trend in strikes is

Chart 3.4 Incidence of Work Stoppages in Canada, 20th Century Overview

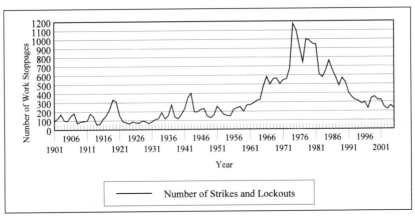

Source: Compiled from F.H. Leacy, ed., *Historical Statistics of Canada* (Ottawa: Statistics Canada, 1983), Table E175–177, and from Human Resources and Skills Development Canada, *Chronological Perspective on Work Stoppages in Canada*, online at <http://srv131. services.gc.ca/wid-dimt/pcat-cpws/recherche-search.aspx?lang=eng> last accessed February 2009.

evident. Although there was a modest decline in the late 1940s the upward trend continued well into the post-war period. After 1966 the incidence of strikes began to trend upwards very rapidly and culminated in the heightened incidence of strikes of the 1970s. Thereafter the incidence of strikes began to fall once again, although the raw number of strikes never returned to the levels of the inter-war lows, especially in the 1920s. As we can see from chart 3.4, the incidence of work stoppages in the twentieth century takes on the character of a long wave that crests during the 1970s.

When we turn our attention to just the post–World War II period, however, the incidence of strikes during the Fordist and neoliberal eras conveys a different impression (chart 3.5). Here the trend resembles a U-turn rather than a long wave. The number of stoppages rose continually from the mid-1950s and throughout the 1960s, and this rising trend accelerated during the 1970s, reaching a peak of almost 1200 work stoppages across the country in 1974. During the latter half of the decade a high incidence of strikes and lockouts is evident, but a downward trend was well under way by the early 1980s. The number of work stoppages in the 1990s is on the whole only slightly higher than the comparable number of stoppages in the late 1940s and early 1950s.

Chart 3.6 gives a sharper appreciation of the downslope of the U-turn

Chart 3.5 Work Stoppages across Canada, Fordist and Neoliberal Eras

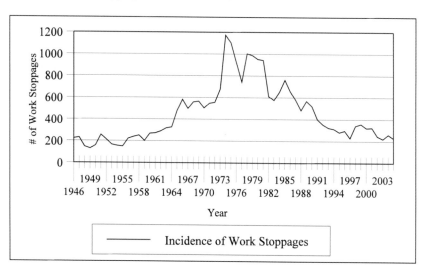

Source: Compiled from F.H. Leacy, ed., *Historical Statistics of Canada* (Ottawa: Statistics Canada, 1983), Table E175–177, and from Human Resources and Skills Development Canada, *Chronological Perspective on Work Stoppages in Canada*, online at <http://srv131. services.gc.ca/wid-dimt/pcat-cpws/recherche-search.aspx?lang=eng> last accessed February 2009.

in work stoppages in the neoliberal era. Since the mid-1970s, the decline in the incidence of work stoppages has been fairly steep. The historic peak in Canada was 1974, when the country saw 1,173 work stoppages, with 1,103 in the following year. During the late 1970s the overall number of strikes and lockouts regularly approached 1000. The peak of 1,003 in 1978 was almost matched with 920 and 987 work stoppages in 1976 and 1979. In the early 1980s, the incidence began to fall from 952 at the outset of the decade to 576 by 1983. After a brief surge this downward trend became more pronounced as the 1980s pressed ahead. In 1988, there was just 483 strikes, less than half of the number that occurred in 1974, 1975, 1978 and 1979. In the 1990s, sharp declines in the incidence of strikes and lockouts continued. Fewer than 300 stoppages occurred in 1995, 1996 and 1997. Such numbers had not been seen since the outset of the 1960s. Over the last decade yearly totals in the 200 range have been common. And in 2006, just 126 work stoppages were begun across the country, the lowest incidence since 1935, a telling figure given that in the intervening years the number of plants, factories and mills had risen by almost 60,000 facilities.

During the period from 1974 to 1985 the average number of strikes and lockouts was almost 900 per year. Over the following decade the yearly incidence of work stoppages fell to roughly 450. From 1995 to 2007, the average number of work stoppages per year fell to just 261. This represents a decline of 50 percent from the 1974–1985 period to the 1985–1995 period. And from the 1985–1995 period to the most recent period the incidence

Chart 3.6 Incidence of Strikes and Lockouts, Canada, 1976–2005

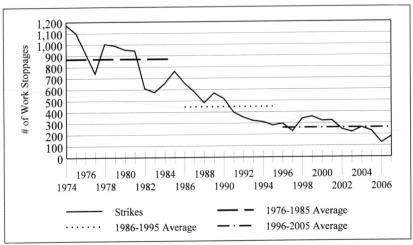

Source: Compiled from Human Resources and Skills Development Canada, *Chronological Perspective on Work Stoppages in Canada*, online at <http://srv131.services.gc.ca/wid-dimt/pcat-cpws/recherche-search.aspx?lang=eng> last accessed February 2009.

of work stoppages declined by more than 40 percent. For the twelve years beginning in 1974 to the twelve years ending in 2007, the average incidence of work stoppages declined by almost 70 percent. To emphasize the dramatic nature of this decline a contrast can be drawn between the peak year of 1974, which saw 1,173 work stoppages, and the low year of 2006, when the country experienced just 126 work stoppages. If we add up all of the work stoppages in Canada in the five years after 2002 we still fail to reach the total number of cessations for either 1974 or 1975.

Why the steep decline in work stoppages in the neoliberal era? One common explanation for the decline in strike activity in capitalist societies is that the strike option tends to wither as a society matures and learns to handle its conflicts in less confrontational ways. The maturation of society, particularly its technological development and its ever-deepening web of social relations, necessitates the development of conflict resolution mechanisms that help disputants realize their common ground as well as their shared responsibilities to wider communities. A mature society simply sheds its combative characteristics in favour of orientations more disposed to accommodation and non-disruptive dispute resolution. As a result strikes are increasingly regarded as a thing of the past. This view dominates mainstream industrial relations literature. One flaw in this account is the transparent ideological nature of an explanation that glosses over the sharp contradictions of capitalist society, especially the intensity of the wage struggle between capital and working people. Moreover, as we have seen clearly in an age where concessionary bargaining has been common, workers themselves tell a different story when they do not opt for a strike, often citing things such as concerns about job security, fear of corporate reprisals including plant closures and general uncertainty about the future.[14]

A different explanation for the steep decline in strikes in the last three decades explores the relationship between prevailing economic conditions and worker militancy. This version purports that the worse the economy gets the more militant workers become. This inverse relationship is grounded in a somewhat romantic notion that workers will fight for justice when confronted with unbearable working conditions and low wages. Labour scholars note that this theory has not been borne out by history. In fact, the counterintuitive and opposite correlation tends to be true. As the economy improves workers tend to become more militant, and when the economy slips into a recession or a depression, worker militancy drops off. Sometimes the decline in unionization and militancy is abrupt, as evident in the collapse of the Knights of Labor in the late 1880s and in the swift fall of the One Big Union in the aftermath of World War I. The lamentable fact is that there is nothing like a good capitalist recession to squelch worker militancy.

The thinking behind this correlation between "the business cycle" and industrial conflict is that improving economic conditions, particularly as manifested by a decrease in unemployment, provides workers with an extra bit of confidence in the strike option, knowing that the pool of prospective scabs is a little lower, that employers might not want to hold out too long at the risk of losing market opportunities during the good times, and that expanding employment enhances all-around job prospects in the event that an employer proves to be recalcitrant or the strike fails to achieve its goals.[15] Research in the Canadian context has tended to corroborate this hypothesis between the business cycle and strikes.[16]

What is most distinctive about the neoliberal era is that the established link between the business cycle and the degree of militancy has been snapped since the early 1990s. Robert Brym's study of labour militancy shows that as the economy recovered from its early 1990s recession there was no resurgence in strikes. Between 1973 and 1986, he argues, the positive correlation between economic up-swings (measured in Brym's study as the rate of unemployment) and growing militancy held. But as the economy passed through the recession of the early 1990s and unemployment fell once again, there was no significant rise in the incidence of strikes. Brym's explanation for this break in the pattern of strikes indicts the strategies of the federal and provincial governments to control labour, including the anti-inflationary measures of the 1970s and 1980s, government cuts, liberalized trading policies and the overhauling of the labour relations regime:

> In the 1987–2000 period, the inverse relationship between the unemployment rate and weighted strike frequency nearly disappeared. The business cycle had little effect on workers' propensity to strike. The reason? Actions taken by employers and government from the mid 1970s to the late 1990s — introducing free trade, cutting budgets for a wide range of government assistance programs, passing laws and regulations that undermined unions — disempowered workers and rendered the strike a less effective weapon.[17]

Brym's compelling argument focuses on the institutional attack on the working class, which has resulted in the relative decline of its power. Insofar as it can be teased out from Brym's notion of class power, we must also stress the climate of neoliberal austerity deliberately forged by governments and materially cemented by decades of intensified corporate restructuring. The very reading of the Canadian economy has been twisted into an ideological message of "bad news," followed only by "worse news," despite fairly sustained economic growth and relatively low unemployment. Prior to the onset of acute crisis at the close of 2008, this message had a profound effect. Working people and the labour movement utterly lost the sense of security that defined much of the Fordist era. Capitalism has always thrived on insecurity, on the threat of starvation that it lords over working people the world over, and this fear of "job loss," of a sudden inability to "pay the rent," has taken a special toll in recent years. A sort of recessionary psyche set in and weakened the overall resistance of the labour movement and its capacity to press for wage increases over and above the rate of inflation.

Wage Stagnation

It is well accepted by economists and other scholars that profitability crises are endemic to capitalism. We also know that capital will engage in predictable behaviours when the profitability crunch arrives, an arrival that never fails. Murray Smith provides an outline of these dynamics:

> The tendency of the average rate of profit to fall can be counter-acted in a number of ways, and the social capital of the advanced capitalist countries can be expected to bend every effort to "mobilize" these counter-tendencies as profits decline and economic growth slows. Broadly speaking, the social capital seeks to arrest and reverse the falling rate of profit by 1) increasing the rate of exploitation (or rate of surplus value) of workers in ways that stabilize or lower the organic composition of capital, and 2) resolving "the internal contradiction" by "extending the external field of production."[18]

The most important point for the purposes of this discussion is that capital will make a concerted effort to lower real wages in the face of profit-ability crises. "Real wages" refers to the purchasing capacity of wages when changes in prices are factored in. "Nominal wages" denotes wage levels expressed in the dollars of the day. The lowering of real wages is, in a sense, an intermediate goal. The evolving conception of work, the fall in the rate of unionization, the collapse of militancy and the reforms in labour law are all wrapped up with this single, penultimate purpose: to lower wages. The ultimate goal, of course, is to restore and expand the rate of profitability. With respect to this intermediate goal of lowering wages, capital has been fairly successful in the neoliberal era.

Over the course of the last century real wages often rose. Sometimes this rise was not so much because nominal wages were going up but rather because general prices were falling. In the early 1920s, the nominal wages were barely holding steady, but prices were falling, and so the real wage rose. Between 1920 and 1924, for example, the nominal wage had fallen by more than a dollar a week, but price declines meant that the real wage rose by roughly 18 percent. A similar dynamic was at work during the Great Depression. Between 1931 and 1936, the average weekly wages had fallen from $26.89 to $22.08, a decline of close to 18 percent. But falling prices meant that the real wage fell just 8.5 percent. It is noteworthy that during the turbulent decade from 1929 to 1939, real wages surprisingly rose by just over 3 percent, a rise outpacing, as shown below, wage performance in the last decade.

Throughout the Fordist era real wages increased steadily, marking the first time in the history of capitalist society that we saw an unbroken rise in real wages across the board. In many ways, this sustained rise is the key signature of the Fordist regime of accumulation. Chart 3.7 provides a visual indication of this upward trend. Each decade evinced a fairly significant rise. In 1952 alone, real wages rose by 5.5 percent and then rose another 7.0 percent the very next year. In at least six different years between the end of World War II and 1970 real wages rose by more than 3 percent. Perhaps most remarkably, between 1949 and 1970 real wages increased each and every year. By the time the Fordist compact began to fray in the 1970s, the average weekly wage had risen by a whopping 93 percent when inflation is taken into account. The largest rise was during the 1950s, and by the 1960s the rate of increase was already beginning to abate. This rough doubling of the real wage meant that working people had significantly more money at their disposal by the late 1960s than they did immediately after World War II.

This rise in real wages begs an explanation. In periods of super-exploitation wages will tend to correct upwards in the direction of the "wage floor," or what was called the "minimum wage" before the latter term came to apply to the legislated rate for low-wage sectors of the economy. The wage floor is basically the amount of money working people need to survive

Chart 3.7 Real Average Weekly Wage Growth in the Fordist Era, Canada

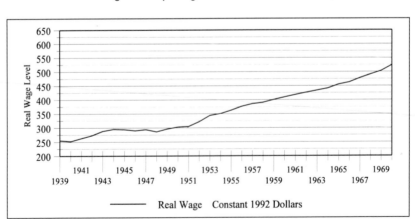

Note: These figures are an industrial aggregate.
Source: Author's calculations from Department of Labour, *Wage Rates and Hours of Labour in Canada* (Ottawa: Supply and Services, 1943), #26, p. 9; F.H. Leacy, ed., *Historical Statistics of Canada* (Ottawa, Statistics Canada, 19983), Table E49; CANSIM, Table 281-0021.

with some reasonable level of comfort and decency. If wages are below the threshold of the wage floor, we would expect to see agitation in the direction of an upward correction as soon as circumstances permit, agitation in the form of increased working-class demands and militancy. This notion of a "theoretical baseline for wages" hardly means that wages must always permit people to live with decency "in the actual world." Sadly, there are many times when circumstances such as a glut of desperate workers, patriarchal notions about women and the worth of their work or just old-fashioned working-class repression, as is abundantly evident in many of the world's export processing zones, permit employers to pay workers less than they need to survive. In response, workers in the majority world often pool wages or cram more than one family into a dwelling just to return to work each day. The term "below subsistence wages" has arisen to describe this pitiful phenomenon in the majority world, just as the term "non-living wage" has entered our everyday lexicon in the minority world. The suffering and social dislocation created by these circumstances challenge our sensibilities. But a correction in the direction of a wage floor will be inevitable the moment a change in circumstances permits working people to apply prolonged economic and political pressure. For example, capital senses that a correction of the Mexican wage is long overdue (as evidenced by much capital flight to China), and consequently it has been pushing for a hemispheric free trade zone, which will allow it to bolt to unexploited cheap pools of labour in other Latin American countries like Brazil. Modest wage corrections in other parts of the majority world have regularly kept transnational capital on the move, with the best examples being the measurable degree of capital flight from Japan in the early 1970s, followed by some flight from South Korea and Taiwan in the late 1980s and the recent preference for Vietnam over Indonesia and Thailand.

The undulations of the Canadian labour movement between 1850 and the inter-war era, swings characterized by rising militancy during periods of economic growth and a decay in the labour movement during economic downturns, can be partially seen as interrupted phases in the struggle to raise the abysmal social wage up to (and slightly through) the wage floor. Research into the conditions of working people in Canada's past confirms that living conditions were poor.[19] This tendency was finally thwarted after World War II, when the altered circumstances of Fordism led to an upward wage correction. The labour movement, securely ensconced institutionally and buoyed by the effects of Keynesian full-employment doctrines, made wage demands over and above the rate of inflation year after year. Capital as a whole, sunning itself in the investment windfalls linked to Cold War militarization, in a slightly more concessionary mood owing to the looming "threat" of communism and, most importantly, enjoying relatively high rates of profitability, consented to these demands begrudgingly. The incidence of strikes tells us that this "wage surge" was anything but trouble free, but capital as a rule could tolerate — absolutely nothing more — the sustained upward wage trend. The resulting wage correction lasted for more than two full decades. As noted above, real wages never failed to rise in any given year during the 1950s and 1960s. An unprecedented proportion of workers, but certainly not all, enjoyed a greater level of relative comfort when compared with pre-war years, although the tendency to get carried away with accounts of working-class prosperity obfuscate the reality for both working people and capitalism. The fact that women were again drawn into the labour force (after being driven out of it rather unceremoniously in the aftermath of World War II) to supplement family incomes attests to the likelihood that the wage floor had not been exceeded to any significant degree.

The Fordist worker had arrived. To work was to be ensconced in a mind-numbing job, but there was a good chance that workers could expect their wages to rise modestly from year to year. Life was more comfortable for the typical working-class family in the 1960s than it had been in the 1880s or the 1920s. Greater wage remuneration meant that discretionary income was growing. Household consumption was on the rise as families loaded up on consumer durables ranging from toasters to television sets. In the 1920s not every home had a Victrola, but by the late 1960s most homes had a hi-fidelity stereo. The rhythm of the year became centred around micro-bursts of consumption known as "holidays." More and more working families owned a car and bought a house. Modest amounts of money were set aside for family vacations or college tuition. The superfluous consumption of trinkets grew, so much so that families would increasingly have to resort to yard sales, rummage sales and flea markets to dump their excess "stuff." At the risk of sounding overly cynical, during the early post-war era the boundless accumulation of capital had created its counterpart in the boundless capacity of working-class families to accumulate a breathtaking quantity of junk. Although we know better than to suspect that cigar-smoking, darkly clad moguls in backrooms planned to distract working people with such wondrous inventions as the Chia Pet, a sense of the opiating effects of such developments still catches our eye and whelms us with an sense of earthly amazement. In the context of these developing habits of consumption the family home became a receptacle for mass culture with its driving message of classlessness, anti-communism and the ever-attainable North American dream. This was the consumptive and somewhat distracted life for more and more working-class families as wages pushed through the wage floor. The hallowed ascent to the rarified plateau of the middle class had begun.

With falling rates of profitability in the late 1960s and early 1970s the mood of begrudging acceptance on the part of capital dissipated, and the Fordist wage trend was halted within a few short years. As we can see in chart 3.8, there was some measurable real wage growth during the transition decade of the 1970s, with the overall growth of 15.6 percent being largely accomplished between 1970 and 1976. In fact, the rise of 5.5 percent in 1971 was the second highest rate of growth in any given year in the post-war period. This was accompanied by a growth of 4.2 percent in 1970, 2.9 percent in 1975 and another 4.3 percent in 1976. But during the 1970s, one of the defining traits of the neoliberal era started to appear. By 1978, owing in part to the lingering effects of Trudeau's neoliberal-type anti-inflationary policies in the face of stagflation, real wages fell by 2.6 percent. In the next year they fell another 0.5 percent. They held fast in 1980, but once again fell slightly in 1981 and 1982. Over this brief period real wages declined by just over 4 percent. On two more occasions real wages declined for several years in a row, with the most recent downward trend beginning in 1999 and lasting until 2004. On the whole during the neoliberal years, real wages have tended to oscillate, sometimes rising and sometimes falling. Since most of the yearly changes have been relatively small, "wage stagnation" is the most apt description of the performance of real wages over the last few decades. If the Fordist era can be summarized as one where real wages were on the rise in Canada, then the neoliberal era can be as aptly summarized as one where real wages have stagnated.

Two related dynamics have been at work since the early 1970s to attack the real wage. One is the perennial struggle between individual firms and their workers, whereby the former tries to drive down wages and the latter tries to push them up. It is very rare to see individual capitalists ever transcending the narrow horizons of their company to argue in favour of wage

Chart 3.8 Changes in Real Average Weekly Wages, Canada, 1970–2007

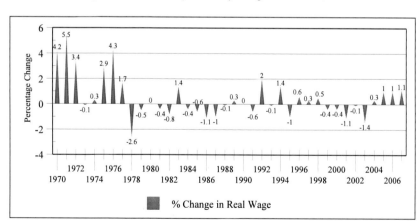

Note: These figures are an industrial aggregate.
Source: Author's calculations from CANSIM, Table 281-0026 and Statistics Canada, *Employment, Earnings and Hours*, 2008, No. 72-002-X.

hikes to sustain social consumption. Most capitalists view wage increases as being in direct conflict with their profit margins. Their sustained efforts on a business-by-business basis constitute an active constraint on wage increases. Even when the climate for sustained real wage growth is encouraging, as we saw during the Fordist era, the high incidence of strikes confirms that no particular company is in the habit of countenancing wage hikes with equanimity. At best, the miserly reflex of capital, born of an understandable survival instinct means that wage hikes will only ever be grudgingly accepted. This explanation, however, is always in play, and thus cannot be seen as an entirely sufficient account of contemporary wage stagnation.

The primary reason for wage stagnation is the concerted effort from capital as a whole. The neoliberal era saw a generalized effort to control wage growth by shaping both the political climate and the institutional framework of society. By the late 1970s the transnational faction of capital in Canada, represented by the Business Council on National Issues, had picked up the corporate ball and was running with it. The BCNI was out in front of efforts to countermine labour's momentum and by the early 1980s was confronting the encrustations of Fordism at every point. To accomplish this task the BCNI led efforts to restructure productive conventions, re-direct state policies and promote an atmosphere of austerity and uncertainty. In this atmosphere company after company was able to extract concessions from its workforce. This rapid assent of the transnational agenda in the latter years of Trudeau's administration gave his policies a decidedly ambiguous feel, sometimes appearing classically Fordist (his Unemployment Insurance reforms in the early 1970s) and sometimes looking distinctly neoliberal (his weakening of the EI regime in the mid-1970s and his infamous anti-inflationary measures).

Chart 3.9 Changes in Real Average Weekly Wages, Canada, 1992–2007

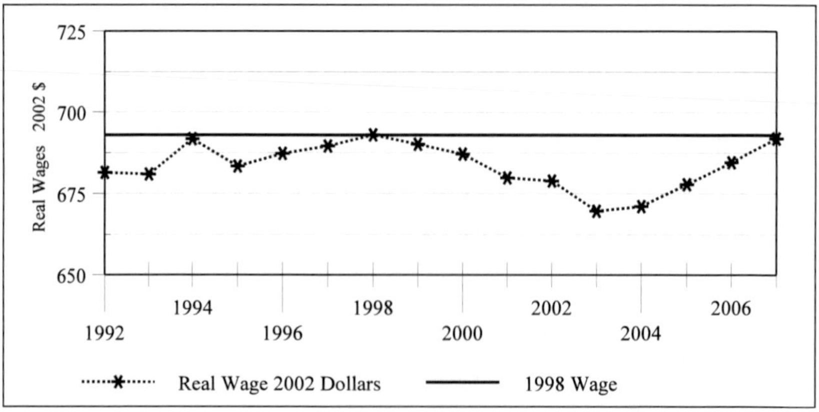

Source: Author's calculations, nominal wages rates from Statistics Canada, *Employment, Earnings and Hours*, 2008, No. 72-002-X.

Although the full-blown neoliberal package of reforms would come together under the Mulroney and Chrétien governments, it was during the Trudeau era that the sustained rise in real wages was brought to an abrupt halt.

Chart 3.9 gives details of wage performance in the fifteen years between 1992 and 2007. Average weekly wages in 1992 stood at $681.44 in constant 2002 dollars, and in 2007 they had risen by 1.5 percent to $691.94. Over the decade and a half they snaked along, sometimes downwards and sometimes upwards, reaching their peak in 1998. By 2007, although they had been waggling upwards for four straight years after falling for five straight years, they had failed to recover the ground lost since the 1998 peak of $693.01. The minor undulations of the real average weekly wage since 1992 are consistent with stagnation. Periodic rises and periodic declines have become the norm. Wages are no longer rising in a steady fashion as they did during the Fordist era.

To get a complete appreciation of the differences between the early post-World War II decades and the thirty-year period after the mid-1970s we can compare the periodic real-wage growth of the last eight decades (see chart 3.10). It is striking that real wages during the Great Depression grew at a rate that exceeds the last twenty-five years. Between 1929 and 1939, owing in part to a decline in overall prices, or deflation, real wages grew at a rate of 3.3 percent. In and around World War II they began to take off and grew at a rate of 20.1 percent between 1939 and 1950. In the next decade they grew by 35.4 percent and by 28.8 percent during the 1960s. And between

Chart 3.10 Changes in Real Average Weekly Wages Overview, Canada, 1929–2007

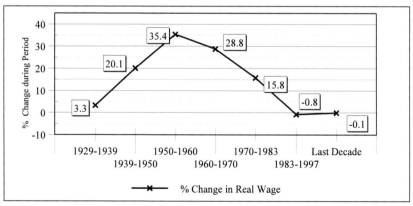

Source: Author's calculations from nominal wage rates, wage indexes and Consumer Price Index. Nominal rates from Department of Labour, *Wage Rates and Hours of Labour in Canada*, 1943 (Ottawa) Report 26, p. 9; F.H. Leacy, *Historical Statistics of Canada* (Ottawa, Statistics Canada, 1983), E49; CANSIM, Table 281-0021; *Employment, Earnings and Hours* (Ottawa, Statistics Canada, 2008), No. 72-002-XX. Periodization partially determined by changing Standard Industrial Classification and North American Industrial Classification System.

1970s and 1983 they grew again, this time by 15.8 percent. But by the time
the 1980s were underway, real wage growth had largely halted, and the wage
stagnation of neoliberalism had set in. The striking graph line in chart 3.10
speaks volumes about neoliberalism's ambition to arrest the real wage growth
that had dominated the middle decades of the twentieth century.

The typical Canadian family drew above the wage floor for a period of
time, but things have been stagnating for two decades. In part this stagnation has manifested itself as a growing debate about declining standards of
living. A sort of hazy politics is played out concerning the extent to which
Canadians rose above the wage floor in the past, or the degree to which they
may have been drawing back towards it in recent decades. On one side is
the claim that most families, on the whole, are comfortably above the wage
floor. During the debate about the Free Trade Agreement, for example, the
corporate world continually reminded Canadians that they needed to be
more wage competitive globally, a loaded claim in the midst of demands
for concessions at the bargaining table and wage flexibility for the overall
sake of the economy. A similar message of wage restraint is implied when a
friend-of-capital research organization like the C.D. Howe Institute publishes
a report, as it did in the summer of 2008, entitled *Richer Than We Think: Why
Canadians' Purchasing Power Is Up While Economic Growth Is Down*. The report
concluded that "large improvements in Canada's terms of trade drive up
Canadians' real income, freeing up money to buy more cars, homes, foreign
goods, and other domestic goods. This helps to explain our relatively steady
housing markets and employment strength, amid slowing GDP growth."[20] The
unmistakable intimation is that the Canadian wage earner has some wiggle
room. On the other side, we see organizations like the Centre for the Study of
Living Standards, Genuine Progress Index Atlantic and the Vanier Institute
for the Family attempting to gauge the well-being of Canadian families. Their
efforts, in varying degrees, stem from concerns regarding the deterioration
in living standards, contribute to reflection about the condition of working
people across the country and offer helpful research that serves to counter
boastful claims about the relative comfort zones of working people.

Recent savings and debt trends suggest that wages have been fairly close
to the wage floor for some time. It is important to note that the flatlining
of real wages in Canada heightens a contradiction endemic to all capitalist
societies: namely that the push to lower wages runs headlong into the need to
sell commodities and services. The increase in real wages in the early post-war
period directly contributed to increased consumption and thereby promoted
capital's accumulation strategies. But in the era of stagnating real wages a
challenge naturally arises since companies still need to sell commodities
and services even though the working class is increasingly unable to afford
them. This systemic tension has been eased in part because working-class

families now spend ever-greater shares of their discretionary income and save much less, avail themselves of easier and easier credit (which the ballooning financial sector has been happy to offer) and work longer hours. On the matter of greater income expenditure it is noteworthy that household savings in Canada have fallen to record lows. Chart 3.11 shows modest increases in the savings rate during the 1960s, which continued for most of the 1970s and reached a peak in 1982, when it exceeded 20 percent of family income. Since then, however, the rate of savings has been falling precipitously. By 1994 the savings rate had fallen to less than 10 percent of income, and for most of the last decade it has been below the 1961 level of 4.9 percent. In 2005 the savings rate was just 2.0 percent. The plummeting savings rate in Canada often prompts concerns that families are vulnerable in the event of job loss or illness.[21] The decline in savings is both reflective of stagnating incomes and likely indicative of the fact that wage rates have drawn back in the range of the wage floor. This is irrespective of how difficult it is to put a dollar figure on this notion of necessary goods and services for the typical family in the northern capitalist countries. The widespread idea that most families "never have enough" or have trouble "keeping up" might be the best we have to work with when trying to gauge the adequacy of income levels. This imprecision persists despite efforts to establish the low-end of the "wage floor range," efforts evident in Statistics Canada's Low-Income Cut-offs or in the notion of a poverty line. The suggestion that a poverty line is the low end of the wage floor *range* is made because no one, when honesty prevails, wants their income level to be anywhere near the poverty line because of

Chart 3.11 Rise and Fall of Household Savings, Canada, 1961–2007

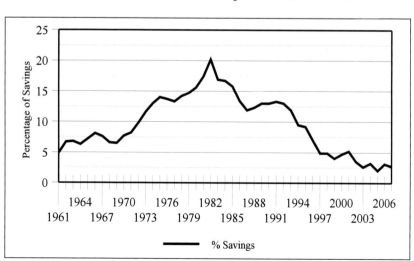

Source: Data drawn from CANSIM, Table 380-0019.

the stress involved in "getting by." It is well understood that the poverty line is a joyless baseline.

The second strategy working people undertake when incomes stagnate is to rely on credit to finance purchases. Average household debt, when measured as overall non-mortgage debt divided by the number of Canadian households, shows a marked increase in recent years. In 1996 household debt stood at $13,519 (expressed in constant 2002 dollars). Within five years this figure had risen to $17,944, and by 2006 the average debt per household had risen to $23,821. The overall increase between 1996 and 2006 was more than 75 percent.[22] A study by the Vanier Institute[23] found that debt load as a percentage of disposable income stood at 91 percent in 1990 and by 2006 had risen to 127 percent. The report also concluded that many families were using credit card debt to make ends meet and observed that the notion of "debt stress" had entered contemporary medical lingo. A 2007 report by the Certified General Accountants of Canada entitled *Where Does the Money Go: The Increasing Reliance of Debt in Canada* found that rising household debt was not a feature of more affluent households, but rather was concentrated in more "typical" or poorer families, and that a rise in interest rates could place considerable strain on indebted families.[24] It is symbolic of the neoliberal era that credit cards are being used to purchase groceries.

The third strategy to cope with the flatlining of real wages may be seen in the growing incidence of "moonlighting." Statistics Canada studies in the 1990s found that moonlighting has been on the rise in recent decades and that the primary reason for working second and third jobs was financial stress.[25] There is also some evidence that people are working longer hours in their primary jobs. One Statistics Canada study found that less time was being spent with families, and cited the increased number of hours worked during the typical workday, which had risen "considerably" between 1986 and 2005, as the main reason for that decrease.[26]

Conclusion

What fate awaits working people given the demise of the established worker, that is, given the fact that the protections afforded by strong unions, progressive labour laws and secure jobs appear to be fading quickly, particularly in the private sector? To explore this question attention in the next chapter turns to the experiences and challenges faced by unprotected workers in the Canadian economy. They have always been there — without unions, poorly paid and fully exposed to the whims of their employers — but their relative ranks are swelling. The project of neoliberalism has been to expand their numbers and insure that their condition is perpetuated. Once again, the capitalist class has been awfully successful.

Notes

1. Figures extracted from *Historical Statistics of Canada*, 2nd edition, Statistics Canada, 1983, Series E175.

2. A good survey of these discussions may be gleaned from Wythe Holt, "Union Densities, Business Unionism, and Working-Class Struggle: Labour Movement Decline in the United States and Japan, 1930–2000, *Labour/Le Travail* 59 (Spring 2007).

3. Sometimes this chilly climate is not emphasized sufficiently, in part because it does not lend itself to easy "measure." For example, the detailed survey in Andrew Jackson and Sylvain Schétagne, "Solidarity Forever? An Analysis of Changes in Union Density," *Just Labour* 4 (Summer 2004), makes little mention of the political climate associated with neoliberalism, although it does offer a detailed statistical portrait of the factors that might be contributing to the decline in union density.

4. As an indication of the prevalence of coping strategies, in 2005 United States Republican Senator Austin Allran called for a ban on solitaire for government workers in North Carolina, a move that would have purportedly saved the state millions of dollars each year.

5. A Statistics Canada study found that 5.9 percent of all workers were absent from all or part of any given week for personal reasons in 1993. See Ernest B. Akyeampong, "Missing Work," *Perspectives on Labour and Income* (Spring 1995), pp.12–16. A study three years later similarly found that 5.5 percent of all employees regularly missed work for personal reasons. See Ernest B. Akyeampong, "Work Absences: New Data, New Insights," *Perspectives on Labour and Income* (Spring 1998), pp. 16–22. The catch-all category of "personal" includes illness, disability or family responsibilities, and its ambiguity is suggestive. As the 1998 study found full-time employees lost 66 million workdays in 1997, p. 16.

6. An informative and thoughtful survey of resistance in the call centre industry by Kate Mulholland discusses many of these strategies and refreshingly draws attention to their collective nature and their rootedness in the social relations of production. See "Workplace Resistance in an Irish Call Centre: Slammin', Scammin', Smokin' an' Leavin'," *Work, Employment and Society* 18: 4 (December 2004), pp. 709–24.

7. On the subtlety of resistance in the financial sector in the face of Total Quality Management initiatives see David Knight and Darren McCabe, "Ain't Misbehavin'? Opportunities for Resistance under New Forms of 'Quality' Management," *Sociology* 34: 3 (2000), pp. 421–36.

8. Research sensitive to the feelings of workers has typically discovered that a sense of exploitation is likely to contribute to a scenario where a worker absconds with the odd product or tool. A rigorous study by Jerald Greenberg found that workers who felt underpaid were much more likely to pilfer from their employers than those who did not. See "Employee Theft as a Reaction to Underpayment Inequity: The Hidden Cost of Pay Cuts," *Journal of Applied Psychology* 75: 5 (1990), pp. 561–68.

9. Bryan Palmer notes that the consolidation of capitalist social relations of production meant a shift from the "riot" as a form of protest to the now familiar strike. See "Labour Protest and Organization in Nineteenth-Century Canada, 1820–1890," *Labour/Le Travail* 20 (Fall 1987), pp. 61–83.

10. An excellent example of scholarly research addressing the impact of strikes upon the social and political character of Canada is Irving Abella (ed.), *On Strike: Six Key Labour Struggles in Canada 1919–1949* (Toronto: James Lorimer, 1975).

11. See David Jay Bercuson, *Confrontation at Winnipeg: Labour, Industrial Relations, and the General Strike* (McGill-Queen's University Press, 1990), particularly chapters 11–13.

12. See David Moulton, "Ford Windsor–1945," in Abella, *On Strike*, pp. 129–61. Of the impact of the strike he writes: "Various labour leaders and other persons involved may have disagreed on the timing, the conduct and the initial settlement of the dispute. However, with regard to the 'Rand remedy,' there is nothing but unanimity in declaring that the outcome of the Ford walkout of 1945 made it the most important postwar strike in Canada," pp. 149–50.

13. The aggregate data on strikes in Canada is problematic. Although I sometimes use the term strike when discussing "strike and lockout data" and although I find the term "work stoppage" ideologically distasteful, this study has not tried to dis-aggregate the data from Human Resources and Development Canada, particularly since the overall decline is more critical and instructive for this discussion. For a helpful discussion of the problems associated with this data, especially with respect to its failure to capture workplace militancy, see Linda Briskin, "The Work Stoppages Data from Human Resources and Skills Development Canada," *Just Labour* 5 (Winter 2005), pp. 80–89.

14. A critique of the view that strikes decline as societies mature may be found in Douglas A. Hibbs, "On the Political Economy of Long-Run Trends in Strike Activity," *British Journal of Political Science* 8: 2 (April 1978), pp. 153–75.

15. One of the best discussions of this relationship can be found in Stuart Jamieson, *Times of Trouble: Labour Unrest and Industrial Conflict in Canada, 1900-1966* (Ottawa, Task Force on Labour Relations, 1968), pp. 452–54.

16. See Douglas A. Smith, "The Determinants of Strike Activity in Canada," *Industrial Relations* 27: 4 (1972), pp. 663–77.

17. Robert J. Brym, "Affluence, Power, and Strikes in Canada, 1973–2000," in *Social Inequality in Canada: Patterns, Problems, Policies*, 4th edition, James Curtis, Edward Grabb and Neil Guppy, eds. (Scarborough, ON: Prentice-Hall Canada, 2003), p. 55.

18. Murray E. Smith, "The National Question: Political Economy and the Canadian Working Class: Marxism or Nationalist Reformism?" *Labour/Le Travail* 46 (Fall 2000), p. 355.

19. Two excellent examples of the literature on the living conditions of working people may be found in Terry Copp, *The Anatomy of Poverty: The Condition of the Working Class in Montreal, 1897–1929* (Toronto: McClelland and Stewart, 1974), and Elanor A. Bartlett, "Real Wages and the Standard of Living in Vancouver, 1901–1929," *B.C. Studies* 51 (Autumn 1981), pp. 3–62.

20. Colin Busby, *Richer Than We Think: Why Canadians' Purchasing Power Is Up While Economic Growth Is Down* (Toronto: C.D. Howe Institute, 2008) unpaginated. Published online at <http://www.cdhowe.org/pdf/ebrief_59.pdf>.

21. For example, see a Statistics Canada article by Raj K. Chawla and Ted Wannell, "Spenders and Savers," *Perspectives on Labour and Income* (March 2005).

22. Calculated from census data on number of households and from *CANSIM*, Table 176-0032.

23. Roger Sauvé, *The Current State of Canadian Family Finances*, Ottawa, The Vanier Institute of the Family, 2007) pp. 16–17.

24. General Accountants of Canada, *Where Does the Money Go: The Increasing Reliance of Debt in Canada* (Certified General Accountants Association of Canada, 2007).

25. Gary L. Cohen, "Ever More Moonlighters," *Perspectives on Labour and Income* 6: 3 (Autumn 1994); Deborah Sussman, "Moonlighting: A Growing Way of Life," *Perspectives on Labour and Income* 10: 2 (Summer 1998).

26. Martin Turcotte, "Time Spent with Family During a Typical Workday, 1986 to 2005," *Canadian Social Trends* 83 (Summer 2007), p. 5.

4

The Unprotected Worker and the Low-Wage Sphere

In July 2004 British Columbia Labour Minister Graham Bruce spoke effusively about job growth in the provincial economy. "Last month," he claimed in a news release, "more than 35,000 jobs were created, bringing the total to 167,800 new jobs since December 2001."[1] He added that "the June 2004 employment level of almost 2.1 million marks the 17th consecutive month where B.C.'s workforce has topped two million." He concluded that "these numbers are good, and show a positive trend in economic growth across B.C.... It's important that we, as government, continue to look for new ways of stimulating the economy because a strong, vibrant economy is the foundation for strengthening communities and families." For the B.C. labour minister, however, the question of jobs was not always about numbers. In his Labour Day message two years earlier Bruce had stressed the need to strike a "balance" between the goals of employers and those of workers, particularly vulnerable workers: "The B.C. government continues to protect vulnerable workers and promote safe and fair workplace practices through employment standards, workers' compensation and labour code changes."[2]

The term "balance" in the outlook of the labour minister appears to be felicitously ambiguous. In the same summer that he gushed about job growth in the provincial economy, the British Columbia Federation of Labour (BCFL) released a study of agricultural workers in the Fraser Valley, focusing on those who hand-picked berry crops. The report recounted the rise and subsequent decline of effective government monitoring of the workplace conditions of hand-harvesters and drew attention to the continuing abuses of berry pickers in the agricultural economy.[3] The 2004 report stressed that the Agricultural Compliance Team (ACT), a government program to inspect working conditions "in the fields," had been rendered toothless in the early 2000s. Children under twelve working alongside their parents was also suspected since the ACT had discovered such transgressions in the past. Other abuses against berry pickers in the province were rampant, including pay rates that fell below minimum wage, unlawful weigh scales that always erred in favour of the berry growers and unsafe vehicles used to transport pickers to and from the fields. The issue of vehicle safety came to a head in March 2007 with the tragic accident involving a van transporting farm workers. Several unbelted workers were thrown from the vehicle and three were killed. The report also observed that many growers failed to provide on-site residences with "indoor toilets, central heating and other contemporary necessities."[4]

The BCFL report gives us a sense of just how stark working conditions can get for unprotected labourers. A study by Josephine Smart provides a direct glimpse into the pitiful living conditions that migrant farm workers sometimes endure:

> Even though the employment contract stipulates that the employer must provide adequate housing, neither premises we visited could be describe as "adequate" housing conditions by Canadian standards. Broken windows in the front room at one residence were never fixed during the entire period of occupation. Several make-shift bunk beds were set up in the basement in the same room where a substandard shower stall was placed to increase the bathing facilities to meet the needs of nine workers in the house. The furniture was in poor shape and the kitchen facilities could hardly accommodate the cooking needs of nine people who all cooked their own meals.

As for the other residence:

> The bathroom did not work for some time when the workers first moved in. The washer and dryer did not work and they were never fixed despite repeated requests. The workers had to do their laundries by hand. There was no plumbing under the sink in the kitchen, two large buckets were used to catch the water and were dumped in the backyard "just like it is done in Mexico" as commented by one of the workers.[5]

Such reports shed light on some of the more extreme mistreatment working people suffer. These reports also reveal that neoliberal politicians (Graham Bruce certainly is not alone) are prone to being both disingenuous and insensitive when it comes to the vulnerabilities faced by many labourers.

In the neoliberal era the relations of power between individual workers and their employers have shifted even more in favour of the latter, a change cradled by a much deeper shift in the relations of power between the capitalist class and the working class. More and more workers are bereft of hope as they navigate their way from job to job. Many working people have few expectations of meaningful legal protections, employment security and a decent wage. Countless workers suffer abuse by their employers ranging from sexual harassment to the withholding of pay. An analytical lexicon has emerged to try to capture this new working reality faced by so many: the working poor, non-standard employees, vulnerable workers, precarious workers, the flexploited, migrant workers and irregular labourers.[6] Each helpful term zeroes in on one or other of the vulnerabilities workers now experience.

This book employs the term "unprotected worker" to emphasize the relations of power at the heart of the employment arrangement. Working people understand their vulnerabilities all too well, but in the neoliberal era they increasingly find themselves unable to do much about it. Everything is stacked against the unprotected worker, and the fear of being out of work for any substantial length of time bears down mercilessly. As neoliberalism chisels away at the ranks of the archetypical Fordist worker, the legion of unprotected workers has been expanding. The pool of vulnerable workers has been growing as companies resort to "temps," outsourcing and subcontracting, all strategies to end-run the Fordist worker and install more cost-effective, profit-friendly unprotected models. Many unprotected workers work alongside employees who are unionized, especially in the construction, warehousing, manufacturing and professional spheres. Most significantly, from the standpoint of capital, the unprotected worker comes cheaper. And more often than not, these workers are female and/or persons of colour. (Coincidentally, as I wrote these lines, a charworker entered my office to empty my garbage and sweep my floor. Years ago, the university at which I am employed, like countless other institutions in the last two decades, started to contract out its cleaning work. Predictably, the former cleaning workers lost their jobs or experienced drastic pay cuts. When the workers held a rally to protest against their severe pay cuts, only one university professor stood shoulder to shoulder with them, and I am deeply sorry to say that it wasn't me. A decade later there is little threat that the new cleaners will ever form a union. The office of a unionized employee is now cleaned by a non-unionized, poorly paid female who is employed by a contracted cleaning company. The essence of neoliberalism just walked through the door with a broom and a dustpan!)

The experiences of unprotected workers occasionally receive attention. The Workers Action Centre in Toronto, an organization that helps victimized workers recover lost wages, published a study in 2007 entitled *Workers on the Edge*. It noted that many workers faced long hours, often took on a second job, succumbed to job scams requiring up-front fees, received little or no notice upon the termination of a contract, received wages below the minimum wage, had unstable earnings, were cheated out of wages and were bullied on the job and victimized by racial slurs. The study also observed that job stress sometimes led to acute health problems and family difficulties. The publication included several revealing portraits of unprotected workers with all-too-typical experiences. The following vignettes are comprised of analytical observations and the voices of the workers themselves:

Raj works 55 hours a week at two pizza delivery jobs making $7 an hour, less than minimum wage. His paper delivery job added another 20 hours to his work-week until he was fired for trying to enforce his rights. His wife also works at a minimum wage job and his three children have part-time jobs. "My eldest child is starting university in September." The whole family is working to make ends meet: "We often use credit to get by." The costs are high. "There are lots of ways it affects us. There is no entertainment. I cannot do the hobbies that I would have really enjoyed doing. We can't spend enough time as a family."…. The stress of this work has already contributed to diabetes and major heart problems resulting in a heart by-pass operation.[7]

Born in Britain but raised in Canada, this 55-year old manufacturing worker had a job in a unionized factory where he was a shop steward. But with closures and downsizing, work became harder to get. Since 2002, Jack has been getting work through temp agencies because "It seems to be one of the main ways of getting work these days." Some of Jack's jobs have been quite long. He worked three years through a temp agency at a steel factory; this was followed by a year-and-a-half assignment at a major retail store's warehouse. At his current assignment at a plastic factory, "some of the temp workers have been there for years. At times they have had at least 100 temporary workers there, [that is] one-third or one-half of the workforce at the company is temp workers."

Zahra worked for a shipping company with other temp agency workers. They worked alongside permanent employees, flipping over and scanning heavy boxes. But the temp workers did not receive public holiday pay, vacation pay, health and other benefits that the unionized workers got.

Sharif responded to an ad for a courier job that promised $500 a week. The company, run out of the owner's home, told Sharif he was a "self-employed" courier. Sharif had to take all the deliveries they gave him and pay his own gas while he delivered packages, envelopes and boxes in his car. "I worked one month, 10 hours every day, sometimes 12. Driving for 10 hours and I spend so much money on gas. For each delivery, they pay you $2. For example, I delivered a package from East Mall Mississauga to downtown Toronto for

$2. For one month, the total they paid me was $526." Even without deducting the cost of gas, car insurance and maintenance, Sharif was paid about $2.60 an hour.

These poor working experiences are common, but we almost never hear about them.[8] They confirm truths about unpleasantries and vulnerabilities in the world of work that are widely known, especially within the ranks of the working class.

The clearest consequence of the swelling ranks of the unprotected worker is the intensification of the low-wage sphere. Low-wage work extends to all sectors of the economy, although it is more pronounced in the service sector. This chapter explores the sphere of low-wage work in Canada, beginning with the shifting historical function of the minimum wage. This is followed by an assessment of the peculiar political struggle to raise the minimum wage across Canada, a struggle shaped by the collapse of the labour movement in the neoliberal era and one that might accidentally contribute to neoliberal wage restraint. Finally the chapter reviews the low-wage sphere with a focus on the disproportionate number of women absorbed within it.

Neoliberalism and the Minimum Wage

The historical function of the minimum wage has changed under neoliberalism, and this change reflects the generalized attack on wages that typifies the post-Fordist era. The minimum wage, in short, has gone from being a device to ratify low-wage spheres in the economy to being a legislative instrument in the assault on all wage earners. As the provinces began enacting minimum wage legislation in the inter-war period they were careful to avoid offending the leading low-wage industries. At the time there was a confluence of interest between labour and small-scale manufactures, who tended to employ women, that helped lead to the enactment of minimum wages. These relatively small industries feared that they might be undercut by competitors who paid even less, and they were thus inclined to support minimum wage legislation.[9] And when compared with the glacial introduction of minimum wage laws in the United States, the capacity of economic sectors in Canada to resist demands for a minimum wage was weaker. For its part, the labour movement had sought wage stability as a general rule, and the establishment of minimum wage laws had been a long-standing goal. There was also a paternalist aspect to these demands from labour, which considered that a legally set minimum wage would primarily protect women from exploitation. When minimum wage laws were first introduced in Alberta, for example, the wages were set so low that it was widely recognized that few men would be affected.[10]

At best, and only at certain times, minimum wage legislation prevented unscrupulous businesses from driving low wages below the prevailing norms of the day. Several employers simply dodged the minimum wage owing to poor oversight from provincial governments. Some firms raised the weekly wage as required by law but then demanded longer hours of work to neutralize the change. The overall effects of the minimum wage have historically been rather limited and certainly did not raise low-wage workers out of poverty. The legislation, rather, gave the low-wage sphere in the economy a sort of legal authority. Wage regulations were set in accordance with the idea of bare subsistence, that wages should permit a worker to meet her most basic needs. At best there was a little upward pressure on wages as a result of minimum wage legislation.

The miserly nature of the legislation in Canada tends to be glossed over by activists seeking to have the minimum wage raised. A study in the late 1990s from the British Columbia office of the Canadian Centre for Policy Alternatives illustrates this oversight. Its authors concluded that the minimum wage is "a useful tool in efforts to reduce poverty and to *generate greater social justice* in the distribution of wages." This is a noble and reasonable goal, but the legislation has never been used this way. The authors go as far as to suggest that early minimum wage legislation was used as an instrument to promote a more equitable wage system that helped to combat poverty. "This latter impact [i.e., greater social justice] appears to have been lost in the current debate," they wrote, "as analysts too often forget the historical reason for introducing regulations and constraints on the labour market — namely, that minimum wages and other employment standards were established to promote *fairer* treatment of employees."[11] It appears that the report's authors have a naïve view of the development of the Keynesian welfare state. Minimum wage legislation in Canada has always been very conservative, employing a standard of "bare subsistence" at best and assiduously avoiding offending leading low-wage industries at every turn.

In recent decades the social function of the minimum wage has widened. In addition to providing legal authority to low-wage sectors of the economy, since the late 1970s, it has become a device in the hands of neoliberal governments to drive home the message of wage restraint. Neoliberal politicians have been holding the line on the minimum wage as a way of creating a sort of moral suasion with respect to all wages in the economy. The minimum wage had been rising in the 1970s along with all other wages, but since then it has failed to keep pace with the rate of inflation. Table 4.1 shows the extent of these declines. The declines, expressed in constant 2002 dollars, extend to every province, and none was less than 10 percent. In six Canadian provinces the decline in the minimum wage exceeded 20 percent. British Columbia had the steepest decline, at 24.7 percent, followed by Manitoba (24.0 percent), Alberta (23.2 percent) and New Brunswick (22.7 percent). The lowest decline in the minimum wage (10.4 percent) occurred in Newfoundland. These statistics reflect the deliberate strategy of neoliberal governments to use the minimum wage to set an austere tone for all wages.

In the process of this historical widening of its political and social function a revealing struggle has arisen around the minimum wage. The push to raise the minimum wage has come from a wide range of progressive forces, and this struggle has appeared in everything from website postings to newspaper editorials and op-ed pieces. The breadth and character of this struggle, nevertheless, is peculiar. We would expect the natural *locus* of the wage struggle to be between capital and labour directly, with predictable interventions coming from representatives or sympathetic groups on either side. As noted above, this more focused struggle between labour and capital was evident when minimum wages were first established. Any sustained gravitation away from this anticipated *locus* of the wage struggle reflects the degradation of organized labour within neoliberal society. The contemporary struggle strangely intimates that minimum wage levels are determined largely through open political discourse, by a give-and-take between interested parties, a contemplative policy environment populated with politicians, business-friendly think-tanks, progressive activists, bureaucrats and academics, with organized labour merely weighing in as a "stakeholder." The presence of academics speaks to the marginalization of the labour movement in Canada more than anything else. It suits capital to have a wage struggle unfold in the public arena replete with a range of views and recommendations. At times, neoliberal governments have even sought to include the broader public in discussions about the minimum wage. Both Nova Scotia and Alberta have set up websites to "debate" the minimum wage and gauge public opinion.

Table 4.1 Declines in Minimum Wage in Neoliberal Era

Province	Minimum Wage 1976 (2002 $)	Minimum Wage 2007 (2002 $)	% Change
Newfoundland	$8.04	$7.20	-10.4
Nova Scotia	$8.04	$6.76	-15.9
Prince Edward Island	$8.04	$6.60	-12
New Brunswick	$9.00	$6.96	-22.7
Quebec	$9.23	$7.25	-21.5
Ontario	$8.52	$7.22	-15.3
Manitoba	$9.49	$7.21	-24
Saskatchewan	$9.00	$7.09	-21.2
Alberta	$8.84	$6.79	-23.2
British Columbia	$9.65	$7.27	-24.7

The minimum wage struggle has the political effect of filling a void, of responding to the displacement of a labour movement, a displacement that helps to blunt the overall power of the labour movement and encourage the moderation of all wages. It is paradoxical that well-meaning efforts to raise wages by progressive elements in society, efforts that are not intrinsically part of the prevailing social relations of power in capitalist society, may accidentally contribute to a political climate that drives all wages down.

There is a second way that the peculiar politics of the minimum wage accidentally lends support to the neoliberal message of wage restraint. Wages of workers are sometimes cast as *one variable* in the overall consideration of sound economic policy. In this thinking prospective minimum wage increases can be played off against other "important" considerations, including job growth, business health and overall economic health. In her discussion of the minimum wage debate in Ontario, journalist Rita Daly spoke to this basic way in which the debate gets framed: "Doing what's best for workers doesn't always coincide with what's best for business. But that's the crux of the debate over Ontario's minimum wage among business and labour leaders, economists, anti-poverty activists and politicians."[12] The push to raise the minimum wage has sometimes been pressed on this risky terrain by progressive commentators in a way that lends credibility to the debate.[13] This pernicious juxtaposition by economists expressly plays off wage hikes, *the one thing that will help workers in a direct and obvious way*, against other "important" considerations. There are short term and longer term messages tucked in behind this juxtaposition — and both fail to centre working-class concerns. In the shorter term, we are told that "having a job," any job at all, is more valuable than having a job that pays properly and permits us to live with dignity. There is a cavalier admission that a low-wage sphere is part of the developing capitalist society for the moment, and the implicit advice to activists and workers is to temper their demands accordingly so as to avoid reducing the number of low-wage jobs. The longer term message suggests that a growing economy will benefit all working people, including low-wage workers. We are informed that long-term economic growth will lift all members of the working class to new wage heights and levels of prosperity and that a low-wage sphere is the brief penance we must endure for long-term prosperity. This is, bluntly, capitalism's other "old lie" — along with the imperialist one that it is "sweet and innocent to die for your country." In capitalist history a soaring economy has never meant that working people within the society are necessarily doing better. A rich nation and poor citizens have typically gone together. Both messages advise that wage hikes, if they proceed at all, should be tempered for the sake of the overall economy and economic growth. This intimation of responsible wage restraint is "neoliberal heaven." It needs to be stressed that these ideas have little to do with economic realities — they are taken seriously by economists because they are in the business of "scientifically" spinning the requirements of accumulation.[14] For small and large businesses alike wage hikes are regarded as a bad thing simply because they cut into profits in a direct and obvious way. The überwealthy loathe wage hikes as a rule and will adduce any sham argument to justify this preference.

A third way in which the gentrified politics of the minimum wage accidentally supports the message of wage restraint emerges as the working class is partitioned into wage segments. Working people are divided into the "have-some" and the "have-not enough." These separations in public consciousness do little to help working people see the common features of their condition in capitalist society. The debate intimates that only the "have-not enough" group experiences hardship, even though neoliberal policy affects all working people. The attack on wages extends to the working class as a whole, as do the generalized job insecurity and social anxiety that accompany the sweeping assault. Any debate that selects one segment of the working class for special consideration risks obfuscating the generalized and inclusive effects of neoliberal public policy and corporate practices on the vast majority of working people. At worst, such a debate can even become a kind of fashionable shorthand to speak about a specific social issue (in this case the minimum wage) without truly confronting its underlying cause (the attack on all wages in response to profitability crises). This is akin to speaking about "child poverty" as though children somehow lived alone (as opposed to the more appropriate emphasis on families hit hard by low wages and cuts in social assistance). The problem turns on the question of how best to capture or describe an issue. In an ironic twist the genteel struggle over the minimum wage actually functions as a sort of political sublimation that draws attention away from the central issue of *stagnating real wages* in the neoliberal era. The *species* (the legislated minimum wage in each province) runs the risk of overwhelming the *genus* (generalized wage stagnation in the neoliberal era) at the level of social consciousness. This effect is likely to be greater in the current cultural climate dominated by a reactionary political temper that is anti-worker and anti-union to the core, and care must be exercised by progressive elements to avoid this risk.

Finally, the politics of the minimum wage paradoxically contributes to an atmosphere of wage constraint simply because it raises the public profile of the minimum wage. As its profile has ascended in recent years (everyone knows roughly where it sits in each province) it has come to be a *de facto* measure of all wages in society, occasioning some members of the rank and file to ask: "Do we really need to go on strike given that we are so much better off than those working close to the minimum wage?" The high public profile of a baseline wage also makes it easier to impugn workers who are pushing for a higher wage. Striking workers in the higher-wage sectors can be made to look greedy more easily as the gap between their sought-after wage and the minimum wage widens.

These hazards of the peculiar politics of the minimum wage are hard to avoid at present. The minimum wage has emerged as a site of neoliberal class struggle, but one that lacks the vigorous presence of organized labour and a strong working-class left. The contemporary struggle has a profile that should not be taken for granted. It reflects much about the times, especially the dulling of class politics at the same time as the class struggle — owing to the assault by capital — has sharpened. The use of the minimum wage as a tool of neoliberal wage suasion has understandably triggered efforts to restore the minimum wage to some level of credibility. Despite the *legal legitimacy* the minimum wage still lends to low-wage sectors, its decline relative to the rate of inflation and its inability, at present levels, to lift workers over the poverty line, has meant that the *moral credibility* of the minimum wage has waned within the progressive community. The push to raise the minimum wage is based most clearly on the widespread view that it is an appallingly low wage sure to condemn its recipients to a life of poverty. At the moment the benchmark that would restore much of this waning moral credibility is in the $10 per hour range. It appears that once that level is reached its moral authority would be brought in line with its legal authority. The term "living wage" is sometimes bandied around to describe this new benchmark. There tends to be less emphasis on the fact that even this re-set wage would do little to erase the debilitating injury created by the low-wage sphere. Ironically, a hike of a couple of dollars in the minimum wage fails to confront the problem of low wages significantly. This point was made with wonderful clarity by Maarten de Kadt in a review of both Barbara Ehrenreich's *Nickel and Dimed: On (Not) Getting By in America* and *The Living Wage: Building a Fair Economy* by Robert Pollin and Stephanie Luce.[15] Ehrenreich's work on the so-called disappearance of the middle class in America is well known. The reviewer began by confirming the spirit of *Nickel and Dimed* in terms of the struggle to get by:

> I have worked all my adult life. I have even experienced a few periods of unemployment. I have always figured out how to make ends meet. Except for my high school and college years, I have never been a low-wage worker. During periods of unemployment, my partner filled the financial gap. In this society, I occupy a position of relative privilege. Even so, with children, vacations, the ordinary requisites of everyday life, I have had to become fairly adept at staying within a limited budget.... It has always been difficult for me to imagine the financial dance required by the low-wage worker even though I am in daily contact with inner city high school students whose parents

are low-wage workers. In this economy, how can families make ends meet, even in the South Bronx, on less than $20,000 a year?

De Kadt then notes that Ehrenreich's thesis in *Nickel and Dimed* is that they cannot survive. Ehrenreich did a remarkable thing by working as a waitress, a house cleaner, a nursing home orderly and a Walmart employee and found that the wages of these jobs did not permit her to live with dignity. De Kadt observes that many of Ehrenreich's jobs were well above the minimum wage. In fact, they were at the levels called for by Pollin and Luce in their book *The Living Wage*. The review raises real questions about what it really means to raise the minimum wage a couple of dollars in one shot. "Surely, moving most low-wage workers from the minimum wage to an earning level a few bucks an hour more would be a good thing. But these higher levels," he stressed, *"would still not result in a living wage."* De Kadt goes as far as to say that the use of the term "living wage is a misnomer." A living wage is not one that frees a family from being "hard-pressed to make ends meet."

It is the extent of the low-wage sphere that merits attention, and a hike in the minimum wage will do little to confront it. Neoliberalism is about insuring that there is no shortage of low-wage jobs and no shortage of desperate workers willing to step into them. The minimum wage is a useful place to start in that it helps us see that the creation of a low-wage sphere is deliberate.

The Low-Wage Sphere

It is commonly argued that few workers actually work for the minimum wage in Canada and that those who do are typically young and live at home. This argument is advanced to suggest that concern about the minimum wage inappropriately dramatizes the reality of lower wage levels in the economy. It also implies that wages tend to rise as younger people gain experience and add to their education. What it glosses over, however, is the fact that many working people labour for wages that are not very far from the minimum wage. As the quartile wage data in table 4.2 shows, it is not uncommon for upwards of 25 percent of the hourly wage earners in Canada to be within three or four dollars of the minimum wage. In Newfoundland, for example, 25 percent of the wage earners received wages that were within $1.25 of the minimum wage in 2007. In Ontario, Quebec and British Columbia, one quarter of all hourly wages earners were within about $4.00. The $5.65 gap between the minimum wage and the lower-quartile wage in Alberta was the highest in Canada. Clearly, a significant segment of the Canadian working class toils away for wages that are close to the minimum wage.

Table 4.2 also shows that the gap between the median wage and the minimum wage is not all that substantial. One half of the hourly wage earners in Atlantic Canada worked within about $7.50 of the minimum wage. In New Brunswick, 50 percent of the workforce received hourly wages within $7.17 of the minimum wage, and its minimum wage rate was the lowest in Canada in 2007. Only in Ontario, Alberta and British Columbia did the gap between the median wage and the minimum wage exceed $10.00. Many wage earners work for hourly wages that are within five to ten dollars of the minimum wage; in other words, much of the workforce is working for a wage that fails to double the minimum wage. Such wages may lift a family above the poverty line depending on the profile of the family income, but they are not bound to render "the daily grind" free from considerable worry and anxiety. It may indeed be the case that few workers receive the legislated hourly minimum wage exactly, but many working people receive wages that are likely to prompt rhetorical comparisons with the minimum wage baseline. An over-worked, under-paid and under-appreciated retiree working in a coffee shop, for example, is likely to think of her wage as being "within such and such of the minimum wage," and the same would go for many other low-wage earners throughout the economy.

Table 4.3 permits us to see that the story of the low-wage sphere becomes even more sobering when differences between the wages of males and females are considered. In 2007, the lower-quartile wage for men typically exceeded the lower quartile wage for women by two or more dollars. Stated differently, working men have a bit more success at pulling away from the minimum

Table 4.2 Lower Quartile Wages in Canada, 2007

Province	Minimum Wage 2007	Lower Quartile Wage	Amount Quartile above Minimum Wage	Median Wage	Amount Median above Minimum Wage
Newfoundland	$7.50	$8.75	$1.25	$15.00	$7.50
Prince Edward Island	$7.50	$10.00	$2.50	$14.60	$7.10
Nova Scotia	$7.60	$10.00	$2.40	$15.00	$7.40
New Brunswick	$7.25	$10.00	$2.75	$14.42	$7.17
Quebec	$8.00	$12.00	$4.00	$17.00	$9.00
Ontario	$8.00	$12.00	$4.00	$18.12	$10.12
Manitoba	$8.00	$11.00	$3.00	$16.00	$8.00
Saskatchewan	$7.95	$11.00	$3.05	$16.75	$8.80
Alberta	$8.00	$13.65	$5.65	$19.00	$11.00
British Columbia	$8.00	$12.00	$4.00	$19.00	$11.00

Source: Calculations from Statistics Canada, Labour Force Survey, 2007 data.

wage than women. In Alberta, for example, the lower-quartile wage for men was $7.50 higher than the minimum wage and the lower-quartile wage for women was just $4.00 higher, a gap of $3.50. The men and women in several other provinces, including Ontario, New Brunswick and British Columbia, had gaps of $2.00 or more. The smallest gap in the amount men and women earned above minimum wage was $1.00 (in Prince Edward Island).

The other striking fact about the data in table 4.3 is the very close proximity of the lower-quartile wage of women to the minimum wage. In Newfoundland, 25 percent of all female hourly wage earners receive a wage remuneration that is within 60 cents of the minimum wage. All the Atlantic Canadian provinces are under $2.00 when it comes to this female wage gap, and three others (Quebec, Manitoba and Saskatchewan) are just over $2.00. Ontario, Alberta and British Columbia have minimum wage/lower-quartile wage gaps in the $3.00 to $4.00 range for women.

Chart 4.1 illustrates the differences in the low-wage sphere for men and women. In every province the lower-quartile wage for women is well below that of men. The largest gap is in Alberta, where the difference between the male and female lower-quartile wage was $3.50. It is noteworthy that the three economies performing better in terms of overall wages, namely Ontario, Alberta and British Columbia, have the greatest gap between men and women in the low-wage sphere, suggesting that a stronger economy in

Table 4.3 Lower Quartile Wages for Men and Women

Province	Minimum Wage 2007	Lower Quartile Wage Females	Amount Lower Quartile Wage above Minimum Wage	Lower Quartile Wage Males	Amount Lower Quartile Wage above Minimum Wage
Newfoundland	$7.50	$8.10	$0.60	$10.50	$3.00
Prince Edward Island	$7.50	$9.00	$1.50	$10.00	$2.50
Nova Scotia	$7.60	$9.50	$1.90	$10.65	$3.05
New Brunswick	$7.25	$9.00	$1.75	$11.00	$3.75
Quebec	$8.00	$10.25	$2.25	$12.85	$4.85
Ontario	$8.00	$11.00	$3.00	$13.00	$5.00
Manitoba	$8.00	$10.10	$2.10	$12.00	$4.00
Saskatchewan	$7.95	$10.00	$2.05	$12.00	$4.05
Alberta	$8.00	$12.00	$4.00	$15.50	$7.50
British Columbia	$8.00	$11.06	$3.06	$14.00	$6.00

Source: Calculations from Statistics Canada, Labour Force Survey, 2007 data.

no way coincides with a lessening of wage inequality. This contrasts rather noticeably with the relatively lower gaps in Atlantic Provinces.

Chart 4.1 also augments discussions about the "gender gap" in wages across Canada, that is, the tendency for women's wages to be well below those of men. A disproportionate number of women work in the low-wage sphere, which is not surprising given that neoliberalism is hardly gender neutral in its strategies and consequences. Over the last several decades there has been a concerted effort by capital to alter the social relations of class power, and a significant part of this strategy relies on channelling women into bad jobs with low wages. Employer after employer takes full advantage of patriarchal notions about the unworthiness of female labour as they slot women into low-wage positions. This process is anything but accidental. It exploits outdated ideas that males are the "supporters" of families, the "breadwinners" who bring home "the bacon" to hungry wives and children, while the labour of women earns "pin money" that merely supplements the family income. In offering low-wage positions, employers fully anticipate that there will be a pool of female employees desperate enough to take the work, and a confluence of neoliberal policies and practices insures that this pool forms. Neoliberalism is about seeing to it that there are enough desperate women to reluctantly fill the jobs and endure the low pay. In this manner women are herded into the low-wage sector, a dynamic for which the metaphor "labour ranch" might be a more apt description than the almost chipper "labour market."

Chart 4.1 Proximity of Lower-Quartile Wage to Minimum Wage, Men and Women, 2007

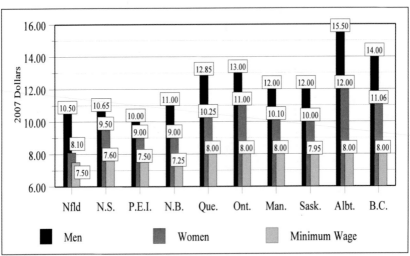

Source: Author's calculations, Statistics Canada, Labour Force Survey, last updated April 2008.

Unionization trends in Canada are also not gender neutral, even though the rate of unionization for women is the same as the rate of unionization for men in Canada. Anti-unionization practices targeted at the low-wage spheres of the economy are bound to affect women disproportionately. Yet another tired myth of patriarchal society is that women are more docile and less disruptive when it comes to accepting the terms of employment. This myth persists despite the fact that it is shattered almost daily throughout the global economy as women resist their oppression by marching, protesting and trying to form unions. Women do not accept their poor pay and poor working conditions with equanimity. At best, and given the hostile anti-union practices that mark neoliberal culture, some women might resign themselves to their pitiful pay and come to believe that there is not much that they can do about it at the moment. Only generalized unionization drives in the low-wage sectors will counter these dispiriting low-wage trends. Unions like UNITE HERE and the United Food and Commercial Workers Union are making modest headway in the push to unionize traditional low-wage sectors in Canada, and such efforts will bear on the super-exploitation of women directly.

The general indication of the extent of the low-wage sphere for women is evident in chart 4.2. Roughly one half of all female hourly wage earners in Canada were being paid within $7.14 of the minimum wage in 2007. One quarter of the female workforce received hourly wages that were within $2.22 of the minimum. This nation-wide lower-quartile/minimum wage gap

Chart 4.2 Proximity of Hourly Wages of Women to Minimum Wage, Canada, 2007

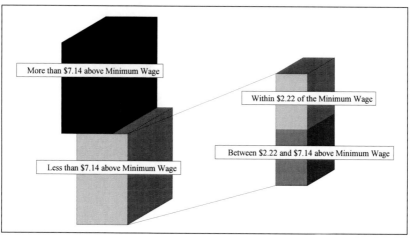

Note: Average gap of lower quartile and median wages.
Source: Author's calculations, Statistics Canada, Labour Force Survey, last updated April 2008.

disguises provincial variations ranging from Newfoundland's astonishing gap of just 60 cents to Alberta's hardly-anything-to-write-home-about gap of $4.00. Nevertheless, at least half of the provinces hover close to this average gap of just $2.22. The skewed absorption of women into low-wage work in Canada reflects conditions in the global economy. Women often comprise much of the low-wage labour force in the world's export processing zones, and they perform a disproportionate amount of the low-paying work in the informal and domestic-service sectors of the global economy.[16] These women typically receive "below-subsistence wages," which leave families struggling through horrendous conditions of want and privation. Although the dynamic might be less dramatic in Canada it is the same basic problem: *a precarious existence caused by poor wages.* Women may not have to rattle their dishes to pretend they are eating Sunday dinner as was often the case in nineteenth-century England, but many are still impoverished by inadequate wages, their lives often bereft of dignity. When women are mired in low-wage jobs, overall family income levels will only be adequate if another family member is able to fetch a much better salary or work longer hours.[17] These "socially insufficient wages" directly relate to the low value placed upon the labour of women in the context of a capitalist class bent on widening the scope of low-wage work in Canada and around the world.

The Low-Wage Sphere and Poverty

The most obvious manifestation of the expanding ranks of the unprotected worker is the growth of the low-wage sphere, which is bound to leave many families scrambling to "get by." The term "non-living wage" is sometimes used to describe inadequate wages in the minority world, and the expression "economically distressed" has entered the North American lexicon to set the "working class" apart from the "middle class." Euphemisms aside, many wages are "living wages" only in the most minimal sense, with the low-wage sphere being an increasingly important piece of the poverty puzzle in Canada. The National Council of Welfare's *Poverty Profile* expressed the problem colourfully: "For some Canadians, having a job is the best protection against poverty. For others, having a job or two jobs or even three jobs is not enough to keep the wolf away from door."[18] Concern about the inadequacy of wages and the expansion of the working poor has grown in recent decades. The Task Force on Modernizing Income Security for Working-Age Adults captured the heart of these concerns:

> Should someone in Canada working full-time for a full year be living in poverty? We think most Canadians would answer "no" to that question. In fact, we believe that it is a fundamental tenet of Canadian society that any individual working full-time should be

able to lift themselves and their family out of poverty. Yet today, nearly a third of Canada's low-wage workers do not earn sufficient income to meet their costs of living. They are failing to make ends meet, not because they do not work hard, but because they can't earn enough to cover what it costs to live and work in Canada — especially in our large cities.[19]

One study on working-poor families found that they often spend more than they make, spend more than half of what they make on housing, food and clothing, rely on family members to meet their day-care needs and forego dental and eye-care.[20] The use of "payday" credit services (also called "fringe banking") has attracted critical attention, particularly its lack of regulation and usurious interest rates.[21] A Statistics Canada study found that low-income families were far more likely to resort to fringe banking and often did so because they were falling behind in their "bills."[22] It has also become apparent that many working people are using food banks. The Canadian Association of Food Banks (CAFB) reports that working people constitute their second-highest client group, behind those on social assistance, ranging from 11.9 percent of their clients in 2003 to 13.4 percent in 2007. For brevity and concision it would be difficult to improve upon the CAFB's explanation of the relationship between food bank use and neoliberalism: "Poverty for people with jobs is the result of such factors as *insufficient wages*, growth in the number of low-paying, precarious, temporary, and part-time jobs and *gaps in wages between men and women*."[23]

Clearly, many Canadians consider legislated minimum wages to be far too low. The *Toronto Star*, a paper that has long-since lost touch with its worker-friendly roots, ran a series of articles throughout 2007 and 2008 on the inadequacy of the minimum wage across the country. The paper revealed that some employers pay wages above the legislated rate because they believe it is too low: "Minimum wage is just unacceptable for families, for single people to pay the bills, to buy food, to pay the rent...." prided the owner of a hardware store in Toronto who paid his workers at least $10 per hour in 2007, "even $10 is not a great wage but it certainly will bring people back up to where they can make a decent living and support their families."[24] Although the prevailing minimum wage levels have lost their moral credibility, even a dramatic jump to $10 per hour across the country would fail to warrant the appellation "living wage."

Conclusion

The low-wage sphere was not created in the neoliberal era, but the goal in recent decades has been to insure that it intensifies, that the number of jobs with decent pay and acceptable benefits decreases and that the number of jobs with poor pay and bad working conditions increases. Of course, neoliberal politicians can never admit this. They have become increasingly disingenuous owing to their inability to speak to the continuing degradation of working life without undermining the essence of the neoliberal agenda. A language has developed that permits them to speak effusively about the economy without confronting the deteriorating conditions of work itself. As we saw in the case of the B.C. Minister of Labour Graham Bruce, they speak of "growth," of "flexibility and "competitiveness," of strengthening families and communities, without addressing the rising anxieties and fears of working people. It is a rhetorical dance that masks the real intent of their policies aimed at weakening worker protections. These political mouthpieces of the neoliberal agenda cavalierly ignore the plight of the working class. Imagine if one of them broke ranks, perhaps owing to sleep deprivation or a clunk upside the head with a two by four, and began to speak truthfully about the intent of their policies:

> The corporate world in this era of heightened global competition is dreadfully concerned about restoring profits. There's no easy way to please them, but we try. They don't want unions because unions push wages up. So we have passed laws making it harder to union-ize. Thankfully, rates of unionization have been falling, but there is still much work to be done. When I speak poorly of workers and pass laws ordering them back to work, I really don't dislike them. Heck, I was a worker once. But I do want to paint a negative image of overpaid, unmotivated, unionized government workers who set a bad example for the rest of you. What we are really concerned about is massive unionization drives in the service sector. We really don't want to do much about poor working conditions and low pay — since businesses would have to absorb these extra costs. Besides, it is much worse elsewhere, and you know it! So work with me, and trust that there are advantages in rolling people out of unionized $25 per hour jobs and into un-unionized $10 per hour jobs. It is all for the best — and that's why we have changed labour laws, that's why we attack unions, that why we use legislation to smash strikes (we used to use the militia!), that's why we overhauled the UI system, weakened social assistance and held the line on the minimum wage. And that's also why we talk about "tough times" in the middle of sustained economic growth — or at least until things really did start to get bad toward the end of the Bush era. We never want you to think that things are going to get too good or you'll start pressing for higher wages — we'd like you to keep buying stuff, but go easy on the wage demands. Let's pretend that the real burning issues in politics today are sexual preference, and crime, and immigration,

and government corruption. This way, I can dupe you into voting for me, cuz I really do take a better line on these things than my opponent. God bless.

Notes

1. Government of British Columbia, Ministry of Skills Development and Labour, "More Jobs for British Columbians in June," News Release 2004SDL0015-000563, July 9, 2004.
2. Government of British Columbia, Ministry of Skills Development and Labour, "Working to Find Balance This Labour Day," News Release 2002SDL0029-000755 (August 22, 2002).
3. British Columbia Federation of Labour, *Hand-Harvesters of Fraser Valley Berry Crops: New Era Protection of Vulnerable Employees*, prepared by Graeme Moore, released September 20, 2004.
4. *Hand-Harvesters*, p. 36.
5. Josephine Smart, "Borrowed Men on Borrowed Time: Globalization, Labour Migration and Local Economies in Alberta," *Canadian Journal of Regional Science* (Spring/Summer 1997), pp. 149–50.
6. The literature is voluminous and growing by the day. The only survey with a coherent theoretical framework continues to be James Rinehart's *The Tyranny of Work*. Other surveys are strong on details and marvelously empathetic, but lack an overall theoretical *account* of the relationship between working trends and capitalism *per se*, even in the era of the Washington Consensus. See Vivian Shalla and Wallace Clement, eds., *Work in Tumultuous Times: Critical Perspectives* (McGill-Queen's University Press, 2007); Leah F. Vosko, ed., *Precarious Employment: Understanding Labour Market Insecurity in Canada* (McGill-Queen's University Press, 2007); Vivian Shalla, ed., *Working in a Global Era: Canadian Perspectives* (Canadian Scholar's Press, 2006).
7. *Workers on the Edge*, Workers' Action Centre, Toronto, 2007. Available online at <http://www.workersactioncentre.org/Documents/pdfs%20policy/Working%20 on%20the%20Edge-May%202007.pdf>, quotes from p. 40, p. 18, p. 22, and p. 30.
8. A rare break with this tendency can be found in Carellin Brooks' *Bad Jobs: My Last Shift at Albert Wong's Pagoda and Other Ugly Tales of the Workplace* (Vancouver: Arsenal Pulp Press, 1998). The book is a compilation of stories about unprotected workers recounted by the workers themselves, and provides sobering insights into work in a parking garage, a warehouse, on a canning line, in a chicken processing facility and in several other venues.
9. Kathleen Derry and Paul H. Douglas, "The Minimum Wage in Canada," *The Journal of Political Economy* 30: 2 (April 1922), pp. 155–56.
10. Derry and Douglas, "The Minimum Wage," p. 156.
11. Michael Goldberg and David Green, "Raising the Floor: The Social and Economic Benefits of Minimum Wages in Canada," British Columbia, Canadian Centre for Policy Alternatives, September 1999. Quotes from p. 1, my emphasis. Aside from quarrels about the history of the minimum wage, I want to stress that their study stands as one of the most forceful statements advocating that the minimum wage should be used by governments to combat poverty.
12. Rita Daly, "Is a $10 Minimum Wage really bad for business?" *Toronto Star*, January 23, 2007. <http://www.thestar.com/printArticles/173845> last accessed January

28, 2007.

13. For example, see Goldberg and Green's "Raising the Floor."

14. For example, see David Card and Alan Krueger, "Minimum Wages and Employment: A Case Study of the Fast Food Industry in New Jersey and Pennsylvania," *American Economic Review* 84, (September 1994), pp. 772–93.

15. Maarten De Kadt, "The Paltry Wage in an Unfair System," *Review of Radical Political Economics*, 36:3 (Summer 2004), pp. 400–02, quotes on pages 400, 401 and 402, my emphasis.

16. One of the more interesting studies remains Grace Chang, *Disposable Domestics: Immigrant Workers in the Global Economy* (Boston: South End Press, 2000). Also see Deborah Barndt's work on commodity chains: *Tangled Routes: Women, Work and Globalization on the Tomato Trail* (Rowman and Littlefield, 2007).

17. See Dominique Fleury and Myriam Fortin, "Canada's Working Poor," *Horizons* 7: 2, pp. 51–52, for a discussion of the distinction between "low-paid work" and "low-income work," with the latter term being more sensitive to the earning profile of the entire family.

18. National Council of Welfare, *Poverty Profile*, 2002 and 2003, p. 97.

19. *Time for a Fair Deal*, Report of the Task Force on Modernizing Income Security for Working-Age Adults, May 2006, p. 11.

20. Dominique Fleury, Myriam Fortin and May Luong, *What Does it Mean to Be Poor and Working*, Policy Research Initiative, Social Development Canada, Working Paper Series 007, (Government of Canada, September 2005), pp. 35–37.

21. For example, see Chris Robinson, *Regulation of Payday Lending in Canada*, A Report to ACORN, May 2006.

22. Wendy Pyper, "Payday Loans," *Perspectives on Labour and Income*, 19: 2 (Summer 2007).

23. Canadian Association of Food Banks, *HungerCount 2006*, p. 40.

24. Quoted in Kerry Gillespie, "You just can't live on $8," *Toronto Star*, January 25, 2007. <http://www.thestar.com/printArticles/174739> last accessed February 4, 2007.

5

Neoliberalism at the Margins of the Working World

On March 7, 2007, a lawyer representing the Retail, Wholesale and Department Store Union (RWDSU) filed a criminal complaint against the Conservative government with the Royal Canadian Mounted Police. The alleged criminality pertained to the fact that the Employment Insurance fund surplus, then well over $50 billion, was being folded into general revenues and not being used to assist the unemployed. Shortly thereafter the Confédération des syndicats nationaux (CSN) in Quebec successfully petitioned the Supreme Court of Canada to rule on allegations that the federal government was misusing the EI surplus. The language of labour in Canada scarcely concealed its view that the government was stealing from working people. Barbara Byers, vice-president of the Canadian Labour Congress, put the matter bluntly: "The reality is the government owes $55 billion to the insurance system and they need to pay it back.... The surplus has been used to pay down debt. It's been used to give tax cuts to large corporations and oil companies, it's been used for all sorts of other purposes, but not for unemployment insurance.... That's money that comes from workers and employers for unemployment insurance. It's not an extra tax, it's not to be spent on other things."[1] In December 2008, perhaps not surprisingly, the Supreme Court of Canada ruled that the federal government had acted within the law when it spent significant portions of the Employment Insurance fund.

An account of the rising EI surplus takes us straight to the heart of the neoliberal agenda. This surplus grew after the EI program was gutted by neoliberal governments and the program was gutted to herd unemployed workers into low-wage jobs. The Unemployment Insurance program was one of the signature achievements of the Fordist era. The litigious battle over the EI surplus came after the battle over employment relief had already been lost by the labour movement in the 1990s. The ruling of the high court in December merely added legal insult to neoliberal injury.

The Persistence of Unemployment in the Neoliberal Era

This discussion turns on a simple paradox. On one side is enduring unemployment throughout the neoliberal era. On the other side is the gutting of the unemployment insurance system by successive neoliberal governments. A basic question remains: "Why is a program purportedly designed to protect the unemployed gutted despite the persistence of unemployment?" The answer to this paradox throws the neoliberal agenda into stark relief. Neoliberalism has taken aim at those sitting on the margins of the workforce, the unemployed and those who have difficulty entering the workforce, without scruple. The cruelty of these policies is sobering, and every once in a while, like others who are not empathetically challenged, I sit back and wonder how in the world these governments manage to get elected by working people, and what the political left must be doing wrong.

Unemployment is a persistent feature of capitalist society. Michael Moore's hugely popular 1989 documentary, *Roger and Me*, the movie that launched his career, drew attention to the link between capitalist competition and rising unemployment. The documentary focused on the direct connection between the corporate strategies of General Motors, especially GM's technological innovation and the relocation of production facilities to zones of cheap labour, and the dismal consequences for working people in the industrial city of Flint, Michigan. General Motors' cost-cutting efforts caused a noticeable rise in the city's unemployment rate, and Moore's film captured the grim social dislocation and poverty that accompanies such rapidly rising unemployment. In one sadly ironic clip an assembly-line worker serenades an assembly-line robot to the jingle "Me and My Buddy." The robot, of course, is about to force the auto-working troubadour out onto the street. Although Moore's central theme exposed the degradations that befall working people and industrial communities when large manufacturers pack up and move, the musical vignette caught the humiliating consequences of technological innovation for working people.

This is an old association. Capitalist competition, technological innovation and employment volatility have been entwined historically. A study of Goodyear Corporation's business operations in southern Ontario illustrates the relationship well.[2] After decades of operation in the west end of Toronto and in the face of growing global competition in the production of tires, Goodyear announced its intention to close its unionized plant in 1987. The announcement came just one day after all Goodyear employees had received a letter of thanks for their part in resisting a hostile takeover bid from the Goldsmith corporation. The more than 1,000 Etobicoke workers were devastated by Goodyear's corporate downsizing. They soon struggled with financial problems and plunging self-esteem brought about by the sudden joblessness — and they were largely on their own. The provincial government's response to the plight of the laid-off workers was flaccid. For its part, Goodyear clandestinely scouted several possible sites for a new plant. It officially announced plans to re-locate in Napanee, Ontario, less than one year after the Etobicoke closure. The laid-off rubber workers were sent clear signals from Goodyear that they need not apply for the new jobs in Napanee, where the company worked closely with local officials, educators and businesses to promote the establishment of its production facility. Prospective employees went through several screenings and interviews to weed out "undesirables" with latent pro-union sentiments or pro-labour family histories. By January 1990, a significantly reduced, docile workforce of 400 began cranking out tires in the technologically modernized facility. By 1993, the Napanee workers, numbering fewer than half the Etobicoke workers, were turning out more than 15,000 tires each day, roughly the same number as the Etobicoke plant at the time of its closure. Goodyear was down several hundred workers and a unionized facility, but its capacity to churn out tires was undiminished.

As these events unfolded employees at other Goodyear facilities, including the Valleyfield plant southwest of Montreal, treaded lightly in new rounds of contract talks. The pseudo-security of the Quebec workers would last only a little more than a decade. In the immediate aftermath of a bitter two-and-a-half-month North American strike of 14,000 members of the United Steelworkers (USW) late in 2006, a strike motivated by widespread fears that further plant closures and cuts were on their way across North America, Goodyear announced that the production of tires at its Valleyfield plant would cease and that the plant would focus exclusively on materials mixing.[3] Significantly, the Valleyfield plant was not protected under the terms of the new USW agreement with Goodyear to limit plant closures and outsourcing. The Valleyfield workforce was cut by 80 percent, or about 800 workers.

This type of unemployment, caused by competition and technological innovation, is so common that some analysts claim that capitalism necessarily leads to widescale unemployment. According to this outlook unemployment is rooted in the necessary course of capitalist social relations rather than seemingly contingent on discretionary decisions emanating from the boardrooms of the corporate world. Long before the nineteenth-century sociologist and philosopher Karl Marx worked out his mature critique of capitalist production he noted the tendency of capitalist enterprise to expel workers from factories. In a series of lectures delivered to the German Workers' Society in Brussels in 1847 Marx observed that intense capitalist competition, in the form of a greater division of labour and the "continual improvement" in machinery, leads capitalist enterprise to turf out its workforce. Capitalist society, Marx summarized, has the "peculiarity that its battles are won less by recruiting than by discharging the army of labour. The generals, the capitalists, compete with one another as to who can discharge most soldiers of industry."[4] This tendency led Marx to reject the claim that there could be anything more than a fleeting identity of interests between the working class and the bourgeoisie in capitalist society. The rapid expansion of the

fortunes of the latter would do little more than enrich the "crumbs" falling to the worker: "We must not even believe them," he colourfully wrote
against the spirit of Cobdenite free trade and unfettered capitalist expansion,
"when they say that the fatter capital is, the better will its slave be fed."[5] Any
short-term gain in the form of employment and wages — leaving aside the
troubling fact that the dependency of the worker on capitalist enterprise
deepens whenever capital expands and prospers — would be offset, and
then some, by the historical tendency of capitalist enterprise to get rid of
workers. As Marx's analysis of the dynamics of capitalist society locked in
over the next few years he outlined a full-fledged account of this tendency
in volume one of *Capital* and dubbed it the "general law of accumulation."
In keeping with his fundamental argumentative strategy that the essential
features of capitalist society tend to create immanent crises, Marx contended
that the "necessary" trajectory of capitalism according to this law includes
the production of a relative surplus population or "reserve army of labour."
Marx stressed that although all sociological "laws" wiggle and squirm about
in practice, capitalism and chronic unemployment go hand in hand.

A more commonly observed link between capitalism and unemployment
focuses on the "ups" and "downs" of the economy. Capitalist history is full
of undulations with respect to economic growth and rates of employment. A
tendency to lapse into recessions or severe economic downturns was evident
throughout the nineteenth and twentieth centuries, and each decline brought
with it measurable increases in the overall level of unemployment. In turn,
this meant a patent rise in hardship and misery, with growing numbers of
displaced workers scrambling to find employment. This undulating nature of
capitalist economies led commentators to speak about capitalism's "cyclical
nature." Many analysts over the last century have asserted that social crises
arising from unemployment can be managed to make them less severe. Most
famously, the widely embraced theory of John Meynard Keynes held that
the use of state levers to maintain the "illusion" of "full employment" and
thus maintain "demand for goods and services" would be enough to make
the effects of capitalist undulations relatively mild.

Canada has seen its fair share of economic ups and downs in the industrial
era, and each downturn brought with it terrible consequences for working
people and the labour movement. The awakening of the working class in
the 1850s was shattered by the harsh depression in 1857. As the economy
recovered the working class accordingly gathered strength, which coalesced
around the goal of reducing the length of the typical workday to nine hours.
The onset of a severe recession in 1873 once again crushed the fledgling
labour movement, and it would take a good decade before the organizational
efforts of the Knights of Labor helped restore the labour movement to its
pre-recessionary profile. The recession of the later 1880s, however, again cre-

ated widespread unemployment and shattered the labour movement. Periodic downturns continued over the next three decades, and each downturn had a stultifying effect on working-class struggles for a fair shake. The Canadian economy lapsed into acute downturns in 1907 and again in 1913. The onset of World War I helped to stimulate employment (a stimulating effect that is at least as old as the War of 1812), but after a brief burst of energy another nasty recession hit in 1920, and another workers' movement (centred in part in the One Big Union) took an awfully hard hit. The slow recovery towards the mid-1920s was immediately followed by yet another downturn, which ushered in the Great Depression of much of the 1930s.

World War II drew the economy out of the depression once again, and Keynes's prescriptions seemed to work up to a point. The Fordist era saw economic slumps in the late 1950s and the late 1960s, followed by neoliberal downturns in the early 1980s and early 1990s. In each of these post-World War II recessions, levels of unemployment rose. Nevertheless, the extent of the social dislocation caused by these episodes of arrested economic growth failed to match the severity of earlier times, especially the prolonged decline of the early 1930s. The onset of the current crisis, however, has all the early hallmarks of the cyclical swings of the pre-World War II era. It is fantastically ironic that the rhetorical rediscovery of Keynes in the fall of 2008 might very well coincide with a return to society-crushing levels of unemployment that more or less contradict the predictive thrust of his writings.

It is evident that Canadian society has always wrestled with unemployment. The problem is not worse in the neoliberal era, but it has persisted. As we can see in chart 5.1, the unemployment rate in Canada has undulated within a fairly narrow range over the last thirty years. The highest rate of 12

Chart 5.1 Unemployment Rate in Canada, 1976–2007

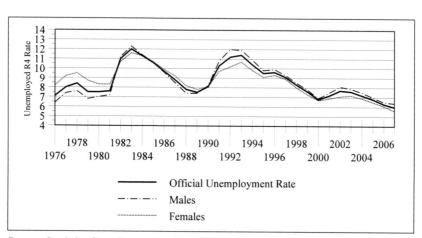

Source: Statistics Canada, CANSIM II, Table 282-0085, last accessed June 2008.

percent in 1983 and the lowest rate of 6.0 percent in 2007 show this range to be 6.0 percent. The relatively mild recessions of the early 1980s and the early 1990s evinced unemployment rates of a little over 10 percent. During the latter half of the 1980s the rate fell to 7.5 percent but had nudged back up again to 10.3 percent by 1991. Between 1991 and 1994 the official rate of unemployment moved upwards once again but declined over the last half of the decade. In the last decade or so the rate has remained below 10 percent, reaching a thirty-year low of 6.0 percent in 2007.

When unemployment is considered regionally qualifications of this overall picture are needed. For example, provincial rates in Atlantic Canada have been consistently higher than elsewhere in the country (see table 5.1). At the height of the brief recessions in the early 1980s and 1990s the unemployment rates in all four Atlantic Canadian provinces were higher than the Canadian rate, and the extent of the difference was often considerable. In the early 1990s, Newfoundland and Prince Edward Island saw rates that were 8.9 percent and 5.7 percent above the national rate of 11.2 percent. The western provinces were continually below the national rate, with Saskatchewan performing better than Alberta over most of the three

Table 5.1 Unemployment Rates for Canada and Provinces, Selected Dates, 1976–2005

Jurisdiction	1976	1980	Height of 1980s Recessionary Period (1983)	1990	Height of 1990s Recessionary Period (1993)	2000	2005	Trend against Canadian Rate
Canada	7.1	7.5	12	8.1	11.2	6.8	6.8	
Newfoundland & Labrador	13.4	13.3	18.1	17	20.1	16.7	15.2	7.6
Prince Edward Island	9.3	10.5	12.2	14.4	16.9	12.1	10.8	3.8
Nova Scotia	9.2	9.7	13.4	10.7	14.3	9.1	8.4	2.2
New Brunswick	11	11.1	14.9	12.1	12.6	10	9.7	3.1
Quebec	8.7	10	14.2	10.4	13.2	8.5	8.3	2
Ontario	6.1	6.9	10.4	6.2	10.9	5.8	6.6	-0.9
Manitoba	4.7	5.5	9.5	7.4	9.3	5	4.8	-1.9
Saskatchewan	3.8	4.3	7.7	7	8.3	5.1	5.1	-2.6
Alberta	3.9	3.9	11	6.9	9.6	5	3.9	-2.2
British Columbia	8.4	6.7	13.9	8.4	9.7	7.1	5.9	0.1

Source: Statistics Canada, CANSIM II, Table 282-0085, last accessed June 2008.

decades. Alberta's official unemployment rate of 3.9 percent in 2005 was 2.9 percentage points below the three-decade Canadian low of 6.8 percent in the same year. Over the years surveyed in table 5.1 British Columbia and Ontario were closest to the national average, and Quebec was typically about two percentage points above the unemployment rate for the country as a whole. A glance at these rates confirms the common expectation that Ontario and the western provinces have been stronger economically over the last few decades, while Quebec and the Atlantic Canadian provinces have struggled to varying degrees.

We gain a somewhat better understanding of the extent of joblessness in the Canadian economy when we consider the "comprehensive rate" of unemployment. Unlike the official rate, the comprehensive rate includes discouraged workers, those who await recall at some point in the future and those who would rather work full-time. The comprehensive rate of unemployment is consistently about three percentage points higher than the official unemployment rate (see chart 5.2). Between 1997 and 2007 the comprehensive rate dropped below 10 percent just once until 2005. Across Canada in 1997, for example, the official rate was 9.1 percent while the comprehensive rate was 13.2 percent, more than a full percentage point above the "official" high-water mark for the recessionary periods in the early 1980s and early 1990s. More than two million Canadians were unable to find a job or full-time work at any given time in 1997. Although these numbers fell over the next few years, by 2005 more than 1.7 million Canadians were either unemployed or could not get the hours they needed. These numbers continued to fall in 2006 and 2007, but have been heading back up with the onset of acute crisis in 2008.

Chart 5.2 Comprehensive Unemployment Rate in Canada, 1976–2007

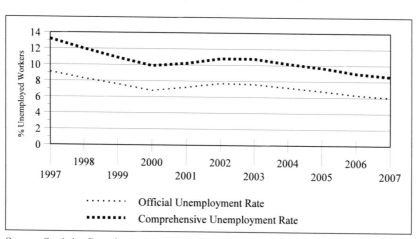

Source: Statistics Canada, CANSIM II, Table 282-0085, last accessed June 2008.

The more comprehensive measure of unemployment provides a different picture of the overall extent of the problem, especially in regional terms. Throughout Atlantic Canada the "real" or comprehensive rate vastly exceeded both the Canadian rate and the levels in other provinces. In Newfoundland, the level of unemployment and underemployment stood at 32.1 percent in 1997, more than twice the rate for the country. By 2005, the overall picture of unemployment had improved, but still almost one in four Newfoundland residents was either unemployed or underemployed. Prince Edward Island, New Brunswick and Nova Scotia typically follow in order. Thus, while the official unemployment rate in Canada stood at 9.1 percent 1997, the comprehensive rates stood at 20.7, 20.0 and 18.6 in the three Maritime Provinces. In abrupt contrast, the comprehensive rates in the four western provinces tended to be much lower than the official rate of unemployment in Atlantic Canada. For example, the comprehensive unemployment rate of 5.8 percent in Alberta was barely one third of Newfoundland's official unemployment rate of 15.2 percent. Alberta's comprehensive rate of 5.8 percent in 2005 is getting close to what economists would call "full employment," and its official rate of 3.9 percent would be hard to best in any capitalist economy. These national variations supply part of the explanation for the migration of Atlantic Canadian workers westward, especially the increasingly formalized system that sees Alberta-based companies solicit the services of skilled workers from Atlantic Canada, sometimes enticing them with high salaries and respectable benefits, return flights home and regular weeks off. In areas of Atlantic Canada devastated by neoliberal policies and industry closures, especially Cape Breton and the north shore of New Brunswick, this orchestrated labour migration, reminiscent of the practice

Chart 5.3 Unemployment and the Seasons, 1997–2007

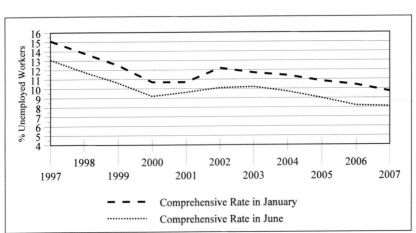

Source: Statistics Canada. CANSIM II, Table 282-0085, last accessed July 2008.

of "tramping" from centuries past, serves as a common source of substitute employment.

The persistence of unemployment is also evident in seasonal variations. Unemployment, like poverty, tends to be more acute during the winter months, owing largely to rhythms of agriculture and construction in a temperate climate. Although Canada is no longer thought of as a "six month economy," chart 5.3 shows that the unemployment rate consistently tracks around two percentage points higher in January than in June. It is evident that the "living and breathing" struggles of working people are likely to be greater anywhere in Canada during the winter months. Additionally, costs for working people are higher in the winter owing to such things as the longer use of electricity, heating bills, the higher cost of fresh produce and incidental costs associated with the Abrahamic religious traditions — Christmas, Ramadan and Hanukkah.

The Neoliberal Gutting of the Unemployment Insurance Program

The sustained rates of unemployment remind us that joblessness hits many Canadians. Although regular employment cannot be guaranteed to ward off poverty, owing to the abundance of low-wage work in the Canadian economy, having no job at all is sure to exacerbate a person's financial troubles. It must be remembered that when a worker enters the labour force today she is replicating the historical dynamic first created when peasants were "freed" from the land and therewith from an ability to survive independently of the capitalist. The newly dispossessed peasants of Europe had to seek out and secure wage labour simply to survive. As Karl Polanyi put it in his sweeping study of the origins of the twentieth century, only the "penalty of starvation" and the liquidation of "organic society" drove workers into the capitalist labour market.[6] Across the majority world today the pool of labour available for work in export processing zones was created by the Green Revolution's mass evictions of peasants from communal land. In the minority world, the necessity of work is conceived in less dramatic ways, but the same basic imperative continues to bear down on workers. This is usually expressed as the need to "pay the rent" or "put groceries on the table" or simply to obtain "cash," but the underlying motive does not vary. As a prospective Sears employee facetiously put it:

> Okay. Start with the application. Start the lying here. My honest (maybe a tiny bit hostile) approach isn't working. Personnel managers, bosses, supervisors, they all ask the wrong questions. Like, why do I want to come work at their company. So I go, well, I quit law school, I have to give back the financial aid, I'm sooo broke, and

they go all quiet. *Like I'd want to work there for some other reason besides the money.*[7]

Kudos, and even envy, to those who manage to earn a living doing something fulfilling or enjoyable, but most wage labourers are just happy to find regular work in light of the dire alternative.

In global capitalism upwards of one billion people cannot secure regular, full-time employment at any given time. Unemployment rates in Canada remind us that many workers are struggling to meet their basic needs and live with dignity. To this struggle the matter of stigmatization must be added. In our Franklinesque world, where work itself has become wrapped up with ideas about goodness, joblessness is equated with idleness and regarded negatively. This cultural characterization can be humiliating enough for an unemployed person, but it is exacerbated by finger-wagging, neoliberal politicians, who deny that unemployment is a social problem and berate individuals who are "obviously" unwilling to be sufficiently mobile or flexible or humble. It was symbolically telling in February 1996 when Prime Minister Chrétien choked an unemployed protester from Gatineau who was chanting "Chrétien, au chomage" ("Chrétien — you should be unemployed"). The prime minister, whose government had overseen the deep cuts to the pogey system that brought the protestors out in the first place, later blustered to the media: "Some people came in my way. I had to go, *so if you're in my way, I'm walking.*"[8] It is this alchemy of hardship and a scarlet "U" that renders the dole unbearable for would-be labourers across the country.

The purpose of neoliberal unemployment insurance reforms centres the grinding truth at the core of capitalist labour markets: work or fall on hard times. People sell their labour power to employers because that is what they must do to survive. If the state were to provide a genuine alternative, such as a guaranteed annual income that would permit individuals and families to live with dignity, many would avoid the labour market, especially the low-wage labour market, for considerable periods of time. Give the huddled masses a guaranteed annual income — also called a negative income tax or a citizen's income — and many people would read a novel, attend a child's school concert or help convert (hopefully unnecessary) food banks into community centres rather than suffer through alienating, stressful, low-wage work. And capitalist censure aside, the choice to stay out of the workforce would have everything to do with dignity and well-being and precious little to do with laziness. Wages would have to rise considerably to entice workers out of their dignified existence. Advocates of a basic income in Canadian society, although well intended and admirably empathetic with the plight of the poor, seem to miss this basic element of capitalist social relations.[9]

When we pay heed to the gnawing vulnerabilities that drive capitalist labour markets we can begin to explain the paradox of sustained unemployment across Canada in the last three decades on the one side and the gutting of the unemployment insurance system on the other. The old pogey system was one of the defining achievements of the welfare state in Canada, coming after the labour movement had pushed for a relief program for several decades. It was only in the late 1930s and early 1940s that a confluence of political circumstances led to the establishment of a national unemployment insurance program. Petty quarrels between the federal and provincial governments had slowed things down, and the necessary political will in the mid-1930s was demonstrably lacking.[10] During the Great Depression many Canadian politicians believed deeply that an adequate unemployment insurance system would undermine the thriftiness of families and encourage intemperance in a manner inconsistent with Christian ideals. Such sentiments, however, were ancillary to the real concern: an adequate unemployment insurance system would actually worsen unemployment by drawing people out of the low-wage workforce. To emphasize the same point from a different perspective, many employers would be forced to raise wages considerably to hold on to their workers. This concern rightly sensed the old truism of capitalist labour markets: give people an alternative to paid employment and noticeable numbers will take it over a crappy, low-paying job. As Struthers wrote of Prime Minister Bennett's unemployment relief policies in the 1930s: "Bennett and his advisors believed that a national minimum standard of relief would increase the numbers of those unemployed. Why? Because wage rates for those already working in Canada, particularly unskilled labourers, had been so lowered by the Depression (clothing workers in Montreal and Toronto, for example, often made only $10.00 for a 60 hour work week) that for a large segment of Canada's working-class a dole which provided healthy and decent living standards would be preferable to work."[11] In the midst of the Great Depression Bennett himself spoke warmly about the motivational benefits of impoverishment and expressed hope that the Depression would incline people "to think in terms of honest toil." Indeed, Bennett feared that the loss of poverty's motivational lash might mean that the "end of organised society is not far distant."[12] The elite managed to overcome their qualms about unemployment relief with the outbreak of World War II. After sorting through the constitutional hurdles, the federal government moved quickly to establish the program in the early 1940s, calculating in a dollar-grubbing way that there was an opportunity to extract more money from working people given that wartime unemployment was bound to be extremely low.

From its inception the Canadian unemployment relief system was carefully crafted to avoid interfering with the harsh realities of capitalist labour markets. It was always a tight-fisted "insurance" system with a restrictive actuarial calculus — direct contributions, specified qualification and eligibility standards, and well-defined termination points — and never conceived of as a source of sustained alternative income based upon some reasonable measure of personal or family need. Its goal was to drive workers back to the labour market. Its most basic principle was modelled after the British poor laws' idea of "less eligibility," which established that someone on the dole should be worse off than someone working in the lowest-wage sphere of the economy. Anything above this baseline would undermine the "work ethic" or, to use the parlance of unemployment insurance policy commentary, act as a "disincentive to work."[13] And so the program of unemployment relief stopped well short of providing a viable alternative to wage employment. Progressive boasts about the welfare state harboured illusions about the pogey system's generosity, but policymakers and administrators always intuited its litmus test: "Does it mess with the incentive to sell one's labour power?" Pogey bought people a little time, but everyone still had to work, and, of course, everyone did work if they could find a job. It is noteworthy that the frontline administration of the UI system was always aware of the need to protect the integrity of the labour market: "If this writer had a dollar for every time a certain UI official told him that the 'role of UI is to give workers a kick in the ass and get them back in the job market,'" wrote Victor Schwartzman in a study prepared for the Canadian Centre for Policy Alternatives, "this writer would be in Hawaii right now."[14]

From its beginning the UI system was also faithful to patriarchal conceptions of a woman's place in the sphere of productive and reproductive life. Its restrictive disbursements revealed a profound indifference to the fact that women typically have to manage a family's way through grinding poverty — a criticism that can be levelled at the welfare state in its entirety. To put this more bluntly, the design of the UI system sacrificed the well-being of women on the altar of capitalist labour markets. Moreover, the gendered notion that a woman's place was in the home, perhaps earning a bit of "pin money," and that the "man of the house" was the "family breadwinner," was a guiding premise when it came to disbursements. After being driven out of the workforce in the aftermath of World War II to make room for returning soldiers, women began to re-enter in large numbers in the 1950s and 1960s. The UI system's exclusionary habits were accordingly challenged, and other issues such as the right to maternity leave soon arose. These challenges led to a slow improvement in the program's treatment of women and modest improvements in the scope of its coverage.[15]

The restrictive patriarchal nature of the UI system was entirely consistent with the growth of the Keynesian welfare state. The programs of the welfare state always respected the need to drive workers into the capitalist labour market, and they never strongly challenged the idea that the man was the breadwinner of the family. Welfare assistance was geared towards rolling people into the workforce, and a woman was typically cut off from social assistance completely when a man was domiciled in her home. Medical and health insurance was never as comprehensive as it could have been, the "old age" pension was always meagre and the "baby bonus" only helped a little bit. It was always understood by Keynesian policymakers and administrators that a social safety net with teeth — policies that responded to the genuine needs of the family and that made human dignity their measure — would have undermined capitalism from a different angle by extirpating its pool of potential wage labourers.

The UI system was slowly and cautiously — very cautiously — liberalized! The most progressive change came in 1971, when provisions were made for nearly universal coverage, eligibility requirements were eased, and special benefits were added for illness, maternity leave and retirement. By the 1970s upwards of 80 percent of the unemployed workers in Canada could rely on supplementary income through the pogey system. In regions facing chronic unemployment, or in places where unemployment was seasonal, entire communities benefitted modestly from the supplementary income afforded by the UI system. Yet in the aftermath of this modest liberalization, concern arose that the system might be undermining the "natural" dynamics of the labour market. Some commentators sensed this but still spoke of the program in a worker-friendly way. Lee Soderstrom, for example, wrote: "When young Newfoundlanders are confronted with a choice between UI benefits and a dead-end, short-term, low paying job, many of them quite understandably will choose UI benefits."[16] But such empathy with the working class was uncommon. Most commentary related concerns that the program had come to act as a disincentive to work and thereby undermined the labour market. Christopher Green's study of the UI system for the C.D. Howe Institute expressed these rising anxieties directly.[17] He claimed that the 1971 reforms under Trudeau had severely distorted the labour market in Canada, that it had become a crutch for many employers and employees alike, and that repeat use and even abuse of the system had become chronic. "Regional extended benefits," which allowed claims to be extended in regions of relatively high unemployment, were centred out for special criticism, and the entire study focused on "evidence that Canadian workers increasingly have tailored their labour supply to the characteristics of the UI system."[18]

Added to these growing concerns was worry about the rising cost of the UI program. As the 1970s passed into the 1980s the unemployment insurance system tended to disburse more money than it received. These shortfalls amounted to several billion dollars in some years.[19] In the face of growing government debt, politicians began to complain that the unemployment insurance program was too costly and that it needed to be overhauled. In effect, governments were once again handed the classic neoliberal pretext, namely, government indebtedness, and they used this to scale back the program. The real concern, of course, was labour markets. The supposed programmatic distortion of labour markets — read a program that permits workers to limit their availability for work for short period of time by refusing jobs (especially low-end ones), refusing to leave certain economic sectors (like the fishery) or refusing to relocate (especially from Atlantic Canada to central or western Canada) — was now implicated in the "runaway" debt of the Canadian state. Anxieties about labour market distortions (the driving concern) were now coupled with the claim that the program was a financial sink-hole. This purported linkage between labour market distortions and government debt amounted to a political double whammy: a state program was wreaking havoc on labour markets and going broke doing it! Calls to reform the UI system were commonplace in the late 1970s and throughout the 1980s. From the standpoint of capital the UI system had removed the lash that forced reluctant workers back into the active labour force within a reasonably quick period of time, and the state could not really afford to be doing this anyway.

And so the old system began to be rolled back almost immediately after the liberalizing measures of 1971. Changes introduced in 1976 and again in 1979, for example, cut the benefit rate of 75 percent to just 60 percent. Bill C-14 in 1979 also introduced the benefit "claw-back" for higher-income recipients. Like many initiatives during the early Trudeau era, the modest liberalizations in 1971 were vintage Keynesianism, but the rollbacks of the late 1970s were more in keeping with the neoliberal framework. The system remained relatively unscathed during the last Liberal government and first Tory government of the 1980s, but discussions about overhauling the program were afoot. The gutting of the UI system began in earnest in 1990. In that year, Bill C-21 established more severe penalties for those who quit their jobs voluntarily, refused to accept suitable employment or were fired. It also increased the number of weeks of work required to receive benefits. In April 1993, Bill C-113 established that potential recipients were ineligible for benefits if they were justly fired or quit without good reason. Bill C-17 in 1994 cut benefits to 55 percent of insurable earnings for most claimants. The Liberals further gutted the system under Bill C-12 in 1996 when they introduced a scaled system of penalties for repeat users, especially claw-backs that could amount to 100 percent of the disbursement for higher income recipients. They also converted the measure of eligibility from a system based on weeks of work to one based upon hours of work. This more than doubled the eligibility threshold for most claimants. And to emphasize the focus on jobs and employment, the old name was discarded and pogey was re-named Employment Insurance.

The clearest indication of the gutting of the UI system is the steep decline in the number of recipients. As shown in chart 5.4, the number of recipients in the 1970s and 1980s tracked (moved in the same direction as) the overall number of unemployed. At the outset of the 1990s more than 70 percent of the unemployed across the country were receiving unemployment insurance. By 1992, in the wake of Bill C-21, the beneficiary rate had fallen to 62.9 percent. Chart 5.4 shows an abrupt break in the tracking over the course of 1992. Unemployment was rising during the slight downturn in the economy, but the number of recipients was falling appreciably. The same inverse pattern held in 1996 and 1997, that is, rises in the unemployment rate correspond with decreases in the rate of unemployment relief. At the close of the 1990s, fewer than one-third of the unemployed were receiving EI benefits. If we examine the gutting of the system from the standpoint of the comprehensive rate of unemployment, an even bleaker picture emerges. In 1997, fewer than 25 percent of the unemployed included in the comprehensive rate (such as discouraged workers or those wishing to work full-time) were receiving pogey. The reforms of the first half of the 1990s had an immediate and severe impact on the ability of working people to receive unemployment relief.

We can now summarize our account of the paradox that has framed this discussion. Unemployment has persisted as a problem throughout the neoliberal era. Yet the unemployment relief program that was established during World War II and expanded modestly during the Cold War was gutted in the 1990s. Only a quarter to a third of the unemployed (depending on whether we use the official rate of unemployment or the comprehensive rate) now receive EI benefits. Why hollow out a program designed to provide some relief to the unemployed at a time when unemployment persists as a social problem? Because the program stood in the way of the neoliberal

Chart 5.4 Unemployed and UI/EI Beneficiaries, Canada, 1977–2005

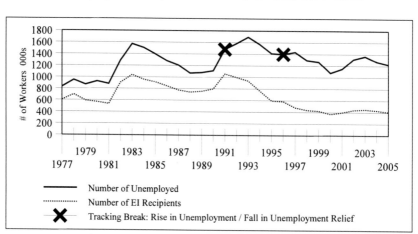

Source: Statistics Canada, CANSIM II, Tables 282-007, 276-002, last accessed June 2007.

goal of lowering wages, especially its goal of flooding the low-wage job market. In the language of liberal economists, the pogey regime "distorted labour markets." It gave workers options, not terribly generous ones by any measure, but options just the same. After the liberalization of the early 1970s working people might be able to use pogey to avoid moving to other regions of the country, to hold out a little longer for a better job, to leave a job if the workplace was too abusive or as a bridge during the off-season. This latitude fell far short of providing workers with lasting alternatives to paid employment. The pogey regime was gutted so workers could be returned to the "labour market" much faster, or denied the opportunity of leaving it altogether. Both effects make it easier for the business world to hold the line on wages, especially low-end wages.

The old pogey system was a classic gain for the working class couched in the justificatory rationales of Keynesianism; the systematic dismantling of the system has been part of the neoliberal rollback. The system has gone from near universal coverage to one where coverage is precarious and unpredictable. As unemployment rises with the continuing economic crisis, the program might be relaxed slightly, especially if unemployment rates reach critical levels. It is very unlikely, however, that the changes will approach the degree of liberalization in the early 1970s. Nor is there any chance whatsoever that the program will abandon its tightfisted fealty to capitalist labour markets.

Neoliberalism and Welfare Incomes

When it comes to those sitting at the margins of the mainstream workforce the neoliberal agenda has not confined itself to rolling back unemployment relief. Declining rates of welfare income evince yet another dimension of the neoliberal strategy to drive marginalized labourers into low-wage work. Levels of social assistance and welfare in Canada, to be sure, have never been generous. The much-trumpeted idea of the "social safety net" has been overdrawn by commentators and scholars alike for decades. As the jobless walk the tightrope of survival, the only thing that has ever broken their fall was an uncompassionate state and severely judgmental elites. In the eyes of the capitalist state, those who remain on the margins of the labour force commit the "original sin," and humiliating poverty is their expiation. Accordingly, levels of social assistance in every Canadian province have invariably been set extremely low in order to force recipients to re-enter the workforce as quickly as possible. In other words, like the poor laws of nineteenth-century England, welfare rates are generally set well below the levels of income that one would receive from the worst jobs in the economy. Terry Copp's splendid study of poverty in Montreal in the opening decades of the twentieth century summarizes the thinking behind this strategy:

The poor posed a problem of some delicacy. A society conditioned to laissez-faire principles found pauperism an abhorrent idea; the concept of making one's own way in the world was the very foundation stone of the social order. Yet, obstinately, the destitute insisted on being there. Fear of social disorder if the minimum needs of the poor were not met, as well as raw consciences, impelled the better classes to provide charity. But, in the laissez-faire context, it was necessarily stern charity, charity designed to be as uncomfortable and demeaning as possible. Such a charitable system would meet the Christian duty of caring for real needs, while discourage the vicious from seeking to make an easy life of pauperism. "Charity, not coddling" was the motto.[20]

The development of social assistance in Canada never rose above this brutal line of thinking. State charity never ever coddled those on the margins of the working world. It was singularly determined to insure that they did not "make an easy life of pauperism." If you could not work for reasons relating to mental or physical health, or because of family circumstances, the state had no other way to construe your identity. From its standpoint there sit the equally culpable — the "jobless," who are not "contributing" and "productive" members of society. The policies of the state have always been geared to make recipients of social assistance feel humiliated at every turn.

The capitalist principle behind this unkind practice is a familiar one. Generous levels of social assistance would incline potential workers to hold out for better jobs. Low levels of welfare were designed to compel recipients to enter the workforce. It draws on the centuries-old recognition that poverty must be the whip that delivers reluctant workers to the capitalist labour force. Those who "genuinely" cannot work, like lone mothers or the disabled, are cruelly victimized by this stingy logic and exploited as examples of the sorry fate that awaits those who do not "work for a living."[21]

Table 5.2 shows these cruel principles being applied in the various provinces. It presents forty scenarios of social assistance using material readily available from the National Council of Welfare, a body that constitutes a sort of conscience of the Canadian state.[22] Provincial welfare incomes are listed for single employables, persons with a disability, a lone parent with one child and a couple with two children. In seventeen of the forty possible scenarios, welfare incomes failed to provide 50 percent of the necessary income to reach the poverty line. For all single employables, the group at which the principle of deliberate impoverishment is most forcefully targeted, the rates of assistance provided less than half of the necessary income to reach the poverty line. In seven provinces their rate supplied less than one-third of the necessary income. In New Brunswick, the most merciless province, a single

Table 5.2 Welfare Income and Neoliberal Austerity

Province	Recipient Profile	Welfare Incomes as % of Income Necessary to Reach Poverty Line 2006	% Change in Welfare Incomes 1989–2006
Newfoundland	Single employable	49 %	60.9 %
	Person with disability	57 %	-5.5 %
	Lone parent, one child	79 %	14.6 %
	Couple, two children	62 %	10.1 %
Prince Edward Island	Single employable	35 %	-37.7 %
	Person with disability	46%	-30.1 %
	Lone parent, one child	66 %	-4.6 %
	Couple, two children	66 %	-6.6 %
Nova Scotia	Single employable	33 %	-30.8 %
	Person with disability	49 %	-21.1 %
	Lone parent, one child	62 %	-9.2 %
	Couple, two children	59 %	-2.7 %
New Brunswick	Single employable	19 %	-17.0 %
	Person with disability	44 %	-25.2 %
	Lone parent, one child	65 %	15.0 %
	Couple, two children	54 %	22.2 %
Quebec	Single employable	33 %	34.4 %
	Person with disability	49 %	10.5 %
	Lone parent, one child	63 %	18.2 %
	Couple, two children	55 %	12.4 %
Ontario	Single employable	33 %	-23.9 %
	Person with disability	57 %	-8.8 %
	Lone parent, one child	59 %	-14.6 %
	Couple, two children	51 %	-15.5 %
Manitoba	Single employable	27 %	-34.4 %
	Person with disability	42 %	-8.6 %
	Lone parent, one child	54 %	-2.0 %
	Couple, two children	54 %	-15.4 %
Saskatchewan	Single employable	47 %	18.8 %
	Person with disability	51 %	-19.8 %
	Lone parent, one child	69 %	-3.1 %
	Couple, two children	64 %	-6.7 %

Province	Recipient Profile	Welfare Incomes as % of Income Necessary to Reach Poverty Line 2006	% Change in Welfare Incomes 1989–2006
Alberta	Single employable	26 %	-23.3 %
	Person with disability	40 %	-2.9 %
	Lone parent, one child	53 %	-4.4 %
	Couple, two children	55 %	-3.2 %
British Columbia	Single employable	30 %	-19.3 %
	Person with disability	50 %	-3.1 %
	Lone parent, one child	57 %	-6.7 %
	Couple, two children	49 %	-8.1 %

employable rose only 19 percent of the way to the poverty line. Rates of assistance rarely carried an individual or a family more than two-thirds of the way. And in just one case, that of a lone parent (likely a mother) with a child in Newfoundland, did welfare incomes lift a family three-quarters of the way towards the poverty line.

The strategy of deliberate impoverishment was not invented in the neoliberal era, but it has been refined and intensified in recent decades. Table 5.2 also shows the declines in incomes for each scenario. In thirty of the forty possibilities welfare incomes declined between 1989 and 2006. In four cases these declines topped 30 percent. In six of the provinces declines in welfare incomes were evident in every scenario. For single employables, again the group with the poverty/labour market bull's eye on its back, seven of the provinces showed declines in welfare incomes in the survey period. Other declines between 1989 and 2006 simply reveal the cruelty of the neoliberal state. In nine of the provinces the welfare incomes for persons with a disability declined, sometimes by more than 20 percent. Declines were also evident for lone parents with one child in half of the provinces. These lone parents are typically female. For them, life on social assistance is utterly miserable as they struggle to mask the poverty of their family in the face of a judgmental world. It must be reiterated that these policies, infused with patriarchal indifference to the toll they take on lone mothers, are designed to drive down labour costs. A study by the Canadian Centre for Policy Alternatives put it best:

> Anti-poverty groups have long argued that changes to welfare that make people more desperate, either through reductions in benefit levels or by cutting people off welfare entirely, are part of a broader "low-wage strategy." This argument asserts that cuts to welfare assist

corporations/employers by driving down wages and providing a pool of cheap labour. This view is reinforced in various IMF and OECD publications — most notably the 1994 OECD *Jobs Study* — that have called on governments to cut welfare and UI programs in order to promote greater "labour market flexibility."

"In popular usage," the CCPA report continued, "'labour market flexibility' is a euphemism for workers more willing to take jobs at lower pay and/or relocate."[23]

Conclusion

The attack on those who sit on the margins of the working world rounds out the neoliberal agenda. A drive-down-all-wages goal rests at the centre of neoliberalism, and programmatic reforms to unemployment relief and social assistance are part of a multi-pronged strategy to achieve this outcome. The reforms essentially seek to flood the low-wage labour market. The term "labour market" is misleading, of course, especially to the extent that it conjures up gentrified notions about our regular pilgrimage for bread and preserves. The labour market is not really a market in the give-and-take sense owing to the profound existential vulnerabilities faced by those who must sell their labour power to survive. The reforms of the neoliberal era have deliberately intensified these vulnerabilities. They seek to drive individuals into the "labour market" irrespective of the toll it takes on them or their families. This is really just a nice way of saying that neoliberal reforms seek to make people desperate enough to take any job that comes along. The best that can be said is that the option of refusing a bad job in the neoliberal era has been greatly restricted, and bad jobs are everywhere. As such, this programmatic reform has been part of a choreographed assault on the working class. So far, the political left in Canada has been unable to stem the multi-pronged neoliberal attack.

Notes

1. Quotes from "Unions take EI Surplus Fight to Supreme Court, CBC Webnews, last updated Tuesday, May 13, 2008 <http://www.cbc.ca/money/story/2008/05/13/scocemployment-insurance.html?ref=rss> Accessed February 15, 2009.

2. This discussion of the Etobicoke and Napanee developments is extracted from Bryan D. Palmer, *Capitalism Comes to the Backcountry: The Goodyear Invasion of Napanee* (Toronto: Between the Lines, 1994).

3. The Valleyfield re-structuring was justified in a manner common to globalization, right down to the refusal to refer to workers as workers. In the words of the Goodyear media release: "The reduction in both capacity and labour in Valleyfield is related to the company's ongoing global strategy to reduce excess high cost manufacturing capacity. 'In today's *intensely competitive* and increasingly global business environment,

we face some very *difficult choices*,' said Jon Rich, president of Goodyear's North American Tire business. 'The decision to discontinue tire production at Valleyfield is one of those *necessary steps* to make Goodyear *more competitive*. This decision does not reflect on the commitment or performance of our Valleyfield *associates*.'" My emphasis. <http://www.goodyear.com/media/pr/23414pl.html> Accessed January 2007.

4. Karl Marx, *Wage Labour and Capital* (Moscow: Progress Publishers, 1976), pp. 37–42, quote p. 42.

5. Marx, *Wage Labour*, p. 38.

6. Karl Polanyi, *The Great Transformation: The Political and Economic Origins of Our Time* (Boston: Beacon Press, 1957), p. 164–65.

7. Pat Pedersen, "Happiness is Pat Pedersen-Serving-You-At-Sears," in *Bad Jobs: My Last Shift at Albert Wong's Pagoda and other Ugly Tales of the Workplace*, Carellin Brooks ed., (Vancouver, B.C.: Arsenal Pulp Press, 1998), p. 135, my emphasis.

8. Susan Delacourt, "Chrétien manhandles protester, National-unity fallout expected as PM takes matters into his own hands at Flag Day ceremony in Quebec," *The Globe and Mail*, Friday, February 16, 1996, A1, my emphasis.

9. For an example of such noble sentiments trapped in a naïveté about the nature of capitalist labour markets see S. Lerner et al., *Basic Income: Economic Security for All Canadians* (Toronto: Between the Lines, 1999).

10. For a discussion of the contrasting approaches between the King and Bennett governments, see James Struthers, *Canadian Unemployment Policy in the 1930s*, Windy Pine Paper Number 1, Canadian Studies Programme, Trent University, Ontario, 1984, especially sections 1 and 2.

11. Struthers, *Canadian Unemployment*, p. 10.

12. See the discussion in Michael Bliss, *A Living Profit: Studies in the Social History of Canadian Business, 1883–1911* (Toronto: McClelland and Stewart, 1974), p. 30.

13. James Struthers' discussion in *No Fault of Their Own: Unemployment and the Canadian Welfare State 1914–1941* (Toronto: University of Toronto Press, 1983) provides one of the best analyses of the prevailing political views and their faithfulness to the realities of the capitalist labour market during the period that led to the establishment of the UI program. He wrote: "By 1940, then, the unemployed had become a federal responsibility in every sense but one. How much they received was still a function of the market. 'Less eligibility' had survived the passing of the Poor Law," p. 207.

14. Victor Schwartzman, "Unemployment Insurance Under Attack," in *Unemployment Insurance: Another Victim of the '80s: Proceedings of the CCPA Workshop on Unemployment Insurance*, September 30, 1981, Conference Proceedings Series, No. 2, Canadian Centre for Policy Alternatives, Ottawa, 1983, quote from p. 11. Also see Schwartzman's piece "How dark is it in the bowels of the beast? Life inside Unemployment Insurance," *This Magazine*, 15: 2, (May–June 1981), pp. 4–7.

15. One of the better studies on the UI system is Ann Porter, *Gendered States: Women, Unemployment Insurance and the Political Economy of the Welfare State in Canada, 1945–1997* (Toronto: University of Toronto Press, 2003). Its strength is the clear link established between gendered conceptions of economic life and the tensions and contradictions that became evident in the UI system in the post-war period, especially the notion that a woman's place was in the home and that the man's place was in the factory. The study shows that the UI system evolved to address contradictions of this nature but hardly perfectly. It shows that the pogey system was not gender blind and includes, for example, a discussion of Justice Ritchie's well-known claim that UI's

discrimination against pregnant women was because "they are pregnant and not because they are women." It also provides an excellent discussion of the effects of policy and its reforms on women directly.

16. Lee Soderstrom, "Unemployment Compensation: A Different View," in *Unemployment Insurance: Another Victim of the '80s*, note 14, p. 50.

17. Christopher Green, "What Should We Do with the UI System," in *Unemployment Insurance: How to Make it Work*, C. Green et al., eds. (Toronto: C.D. Howe Institute, 1994). This study formed part of the Institute's "Social Policy Challenge" series. It produced another title that focused exclusively on Atlantic Canada, Doug May and Alton Hollet, *The Rock and a Hard Place: Atlantic Canada and the UI Trap* (Toronto: C.D. Howe Institute, 1995). Not surprisingly, the study often focused on distortions to the labour market, by which was meant *inter alia* that workers would remain in industries where work was scarce and irregular. See, for example, the discussion of the fishing industry, Chapter 3, pp. 62–89.

18. Green, p. 2.

19. See the chart for 1976–1996 in Zhengxi Lin, "Employment Insurance in Canada: Policy Changes," *Perspectives on Labour and Income*, Summer 1998 (Ottawa: Statistics Canada), p. 42.

20. Terry Copp, *The Anatomy of Poverty: The Condition of the Working Class in Montreal, 1897–1929* (Toronto, Ontario: McClelland and Stewart, 1974), p. 106.

21. As an example of this tendency see Margaret Little, *No Car, No Radio, No Liquor Permit: The Moral Regulation of Single Mothers in Ontario, 1920–1997* (Oxford University Press, Toronto, 1998).

22. Data compiled from National Council of Welfare, *Welfare Incomes 2006/2007* Volume 128 (Winter 2008). Available at <http://www.ncwcnbes.net/documents/researchpublications/OtherPublications/2008Report-WelfareIncomes2006-2007/Report-WelfareIncomes2006-2007E.pdf> Accessed January 2009.

23. See Seth Klein and Barbara Montgomery, *Depressing Wages: Why Welfare Cuts Hurt Both the Welfare and the Working Poor*, British Columbia: Canadian Centre for Policy Alternatives, (March 2001), quote from p. 5.

6

Restoring the Canadian Left

In the fall of 2008 the global capitalist system was confronted with a major crisis, which was manifested in falling stock markets, collapsing financial institutions, the tightening up of credit, a bankrupt auto industry and steep declines in commodity prices. By most accounts the economy was heading into a long-term recession and unemployment rates were rising quickly. Commentators drew parallels with the 1930s and talked of a new "new deal." Suddenly, Keynes was in; Friedman was out; and Galbraith's "affluent society" looked to be taking an awful hit. Demand-management policies and government stimulus packages, sometimes even with the Keynesian label, were all the rage again. (Of course, when it came to such things as military spending and taxes for most working people, Keynesianism had never passed.) "Regulation" was no longer a dirty word, and unqualified support for free markets was rejected in Obama's 2009 inaugural address, ironically just as the controversial Milton Friedman Institute was getting off the ground at the University of Chicago. In Canada, Prime Minister Harper advised that he would not be too worried about running deficits if the economy truly needed government stimulation. Neoliberalism seemed dead or, at least, *free marketism* was being ignominiously repudiated in much of the world.

With neoliberalism fading as the preferred idiom of capital accumulation a new regime of growth is bound to emerge. What has tended to go unnoticed in both Canada and the United States, however, is the troubling fact that the so-called "new deal" of the 1930s was forged with the presence of an energetic left, at a time when the system itself was seen to be under threat from communism. This configuration of class relations and historical tides no longer holds true. As a new regime of accumulation takes shape the voice of the working class will be muted owing to the sorry state of the left in Canada. The post-neoliberal era, therefore, will not be kinder to working people. Optimism that the new regime will better insulate working people from the ravages of unfettered accumulation, like a pendulum swinging back in their favour, is rooted in a naïve view of class struggle. There is no such thing as beneficent politics when it comes to the capitalist class — the ever-pressing logics of competition deaden any instinct to be generous, and capitalists are not blessed with more generosity than other mortals.

The factions of capital will broker a new "new deal" that will contain just enough "good will" to save "the system." The new era in North America will be fashioned largely by the requirements of capital accumulation, and labour is not about to fair any better than it has in recent decades. Said a little differently, there will be no Rooseveltian "new dealer" in the post-Bush era because the left has crumbled. Capital will forge a new economic framework, and labour, after years of neoliberal hammering, will demur mildly and provide *pro forma* ratification. The central point is that the new compromise setting the revised institutional terms of accumulation will retain all of neoliberalism's regressive features pertaining to labour. During the worst part of the crisis the "pogey" may loosen ever so slightly, real wages may rise owing to deflation and government-sponsored economic initiatives may create jobs, but the neoliberal screws will continue to tighten for the working class all the same. Those aspects of the neoliberal paradigm that declawed the working class and fundamentally altered the social relations of power in favour of capital are not about to be dismantled any time soon. Only pressure by labour and the left will do this, and the labour movement and the left are in a bad way.

This point about the strange politics of the present conjuncture is worth reiterating. As the neoliberal era enters its twilight it is hard to imagine that the left will have much of a role in shaping the post-neoliberal "Promised Land." The new order will emerge slowly and will likely include enough "regulation" so the assorted factions of capital do not devour each other in the drive to accumulate. But the basket of anti-worker measures, sometimes referred to as the deregulation of labour markets, is unlikely to fade away. Any reversal of the anti-worker measures will occur only when there is a resurgent left.

Prior to exploring ways to rebuild the left in Canada we must first focus attention on the present character of the left, particularly its outlook on capitalism. Accordingly, this chapter first provides an assessment of the progressive left in Canada today. The chapter then explores suggestions about restoring the Canadian left.

The Left in Canada Today

To gain some sense of how best to re-ignite the left, we must begin with a question: What is the left? The American philosopher and social critic Richard Rorty offered as good a definition as anyone when he claimed that the left does not think that the world in its current state is acceptable and thus seeks to make it more just.[1] The left, as a movement, is comprised of people who are not satisfied with many features of contemporary life — its poverty, its abuses of working people, its wars, its environmental degradation and so forth. Their empathy for those who suffer is a rebel passion. They are frustrated by the capacity of mainstream society to ignore suffering and wary of political and economic promises that things will improve over time. Their unease leads them to vote for political parties with sympathetic platforms, send money to organizations that confront the dispiriting aspects of the world, join demonstrations, volunteer and generally try to turn the world into something better. They desire to see the world become fairer and more just and would, as the twentieth-century philosopher Alfred North Whitehead professed when defining the very meaning of "civilization," generally like to see the salient use of "force" be replaced by the use of "persuasion." Empathy and dogged determination mark the progressive spirit.

There is, however, another way to define the left, which has to do with the ancient notion of critique. For many ancients things could be both true and false at the same time. To be critical meant that a person could hold that the very real world, full of tangible practices and conventions, could still be unreal and untrue — that is, not in keeping with the proper order of things, not really faithful to the way things are supposed to be. As Athens was amassing its empire and heading into war with Sparta and its allies, many Greek intellectuals, including Thucydides the historian, Aristophanes the comic poet and Euripides the tragedian, all stressed that the world was unfolding in a manner that was not true to the way it should be, not in keeping with the proper order of things, namely, peacefulness. The Peloponnesian War spanned an entire generation; it was very real, but it was also awfully wrong and untrue to "the good life."

For the left "to be critical" in this sense requires it to embrace the view that the very basic organization of capitalist society fails to be in keeping with the *proper order of things*. Capitalism — its alienating character, its devastating ecological practices, its obscene extremes of wealth and poverty, its tendencies towards universal commodification, its propensity for war and its sheer wastefulness, to say nothing of its capacity to create crisis after crisis, simply cannot be squared with "the good life" in any Aristotelean sense of the term. A critical left would harbour a deep suspicion about the nature of capitalism itself. The left would see capitalism's essential, defining features as flawed and accordingly would strongly suspect capitalism of necessarily immuring humanity in never ending misery and privation. Such a left would push to see capitalism consigned to the proverbial scrapheap of history.

Bearing in mind that two measures of the left are possible, we can explore the nature of the left in Canada today by posing further questions: Does the anti-neoliberal movement in Canada actually serve to strengthen the very forces that undergird neoliberalism and capitalist globalization in the first place? As the left strives to humanize capitalism, to sand down its rough edges, is a life dominated by capitalist social relations tacitly assumed to be the only possible world? To express this question in terms characteristic of the hubris of the early 1990s and the heralded writings of Francis Fukuyama, does the anti-neoliberal movement merely wish to gentrify the apparent "end of history"? Are we in the midst of an historic political struggle that sees, on one side, unrelenting pressure for relatively unfettered global capitalism and its promise to bring "the greatest advantage to the greatest number of people" confronting, on the other side, a progressive movement that also assumes a world dominated by capitalist social relations but insists that these basic relations be infused with considerations of fairness, justice and environmental responsibility? Or, is it the case that capitalism itself — a system of private property, wage labour and highly developed market relations — is no longer "on the table" or "up for debate"?

Such queries illuminate my claim that the prevailing left in Canada does not reject capitalism. This progressive force is noteworthy for its refusal to entertain alternative social vistas. It is characterized by the collapse of any standpoints that explicitly repudiate capitalist social relations. For this left, the world that stands before us is not "untrue" but rather in need of "tweaking." In more analytical language, political life in Canada has lost the *negating* reflex, the reflex that turns away from the basic social relations of capitalism. In a Canada where poverty is on the rise, where working people are being hammered from countless directions and where a new Canadian-style militarism seems to be orchestrating its own birth, capitalism itself is taken to be sacrosanct. Almost all voices of criticism and dissent call for something friendlier, something less cruel, less humiliating and even less violent, but something that is, when all is said and done, *capitalist* nevertheless.[2] The consensual elements in political discourse between the "left" and the "right" in Canada are striking. These opposing political forces agree on the economic fundamentals. This fundamental consensus has tamed a more severely critical attitude. Ironically, as the decades have passed and things have gotten worse by any standard of suffering in Canada and around the world, the view that capitalism itself might be the problem has tended to wither.

This claim is a bit overdrawn. The instinct to reject elements of capitalism may have petered out on the left, but people vote with their feet and reject capitalist society everywhere. On the ground a veritable "second society" dwells in the shadows of the "first society," a society that tends to stay off the radar screens of the mainstream media and leading political groups. This is the society that has "removed itself, thank you" from the primary capitalist world. Its citizens seek to sidestep capitalism's exploitative tendencies, its hectic rhythms of daily life and its poignant contradictions. The logical line of demarcation is the habit of rejecting some or all of the practices of capitalism. They do not merely despise the "spirit of the capitalist" in its vague, Weberian sense, but rather turn away from its essential social relations centred around wage labour, private property and universal commodification. The second society seeks to carve out a mode of survival that is less rushed, much more human-needs-oriented, more in tune with the natural and spiritual world and, to be sure, peaceful. Over the years it has included barter communities, minimalist movements, communal societies, religious communities, back-to-the-landers, co-operative communities and a legion of concerned volunteers.[3]

The populace of the second society includes many who were born into an alternative community established by earlier generations. The second society, however, also includes scores of tortured souls who have repudiated many of the principles and institutions of the first society. They strive to find a community that is organic and internally true to the authentic demands of life, and avoid as much as possible participation in communities that feel voluntary and external; they seek *to be* a part of a community rather than merely *joining* one. They often tend not to "make a living" but rather piece an existence together that is relatively free from emotional distress and complications of conscience associated with the daily routines of the first society. At a time when the burdens of modernity render the task of daily life more challenging for everyone, especially by creating the possibility of "guilt" and "shame" arising from the simplest of tasks like grocery shopping, driving to work or watching television, it has managed to select out a special brand of absolute sufferers who must "drop out" of mainstream society, in whole or in part, just to cope. These are the anguished denizens of the second society.

In the second society resides what some might call the "genuine moment of criticism." Like the ancients who associated the very idea of critique with the notion that the world before them was false, so the citizens of the second society fold their arms, turn away and declare: "No!" They reject the world and seek to live another way, for the world before them does not feel proper. When considered against the last few decades they make our one-dimensional world feel a little less flat in the Marcusean sense. To a man or woman they will find the musings of Henry David Thoreau solacing and the success-oriented councils of Ben Franklin's autobiography borderline pathological. To fit in would be, for them, the mark of failure; they live in fear at being sucked into the vortex of the prevailing capitalist world.

But in the second society the possibility of political transformation fails to develop and mature. The second society is not part of the *political life force* of society, a fact that prompted G.W.F. Hegel's harsh indictment of the Quakers so long ago. The routines of this rejectionist society may constitute the "embryo of the future within the old," as Marx once speculated when speaking about cooperatives, but it is unclear how their alternative modes of existence can do anything but remain on the margins of the mainstream world. This has been especially true for the self-contained religious communities across Canada. Nothing has really changed in the intervening decades since Hegel's unsparing assessment of the Quakers. The second society tends not to contribute to the political life-blood of society in any meaningful way. These "conscientious objectors" chisel away at the main features of capitalist society by refusing to buy things, give away their superfluous possessions, return to the land alone or as part of a collective, volunteer for long hours to make the world a better place and so forth. The mainstream left offers little political sanctuary for these natives of negation owing to the fact that it does not reject the essential aspects of capitalism — private property, wage labour and universal commodification. The odd member of the *second society* might dilly-dally among the ranks of the mainstream left in body, but never in spirit. The political world offers them no home and little solace. The citizens of the second society pursue small-scale perfections in a world that feels upside-down and alienating, and the left-right politics of capitalist preservation are not about to make them feel much better. But neither is their "example" going to change the world. From the standpoint of the politics of class and the evolution of capitalism, the presence of *islands of integrity* within the *ocean of capitalism* will never ever develop into a meaningful, transformative political force.

Although the instinct to negate is hardly dead in Canadian society, it does not form a part of the left, nor is it likely to steer political struggle in the direction of a post-capitalist world. And so we can return to the principal claim about the left in Canada today, where any flame of anti-capitalism has long since been extinguished. The left is estranged from the Trotskyist and communist currents of Marxism in Canada and meshes awkwardly with the editorial line of publications such as *Canadian Dimension*. The left does not reject the core of the world that stands before it, but rather rejects selected aspects of the world in favour of something more bearable — fair profits over unrestrained corporate accumulation, universal standards of well-being against poverty and sustainable development rather than environmental degradation. This left is the product of a long journey from the Knights of Labor to the NDP, the Council of Canadians and the Green Party, a journey that passed through anti-communist hysteria and the CCF along the way. In this left resides the spirit of reform and renewal. In a sense the defining political moment of this progressive movement occurred when the NDP removed its opposition to capitalism in its founding manifesto.[4]

In the left today we witness a wholesale immersion in the immediacies of capitalist life and its pathologies — a ravaged natural world, chronic joblessness and poverty, peacelessness, money-grubbing corporate profiteering of the most conspicuous sort — so that the *critical attitude* succumbs wholly to the desire to see this or that ugly trend ameliorated without delay. Progressive commentators weigh in on the cruelty of the day and insist on appropriate policy changes. The left would like to see welfare policies reformed in a manner that does not involve cutting payments, it would like to see the unemployment insurance system restored, it would like to see public health care preserved and privatization resisted, it would like to see the minimum wage raised, a greater regulation of corporate practices, the greening of capitalist enterprise and so forth. It believes that neoliberal policies have been far too harmful to far too many people and that remedial action must be taken now. In the end the progressive movement in Canada both *is* and *is not* optimistic; it believes wholeheartedly that capitalism is retrievable with appropriately deployed government intervention and regulation (the optimistic part), but it also calls for immediate attention to the staggering human costs and horrendous environmental tolls (the pessimistic part).

The measure of politics for the left in Canada is often little more than a Panglossian take on the "golden age" of capitalism. The problem is *bad capitalism* rather than capitalism itself. The mainstream left lacks a core critique derived from a coherent inquiry into the nature of capitalism *per se*, just as it lacks a long-range understanding of human sociocultural evolution that ever gets beyond the vacuity of Karl Popper's ideas about "piecemeal engineering" in democratic societies. The left is progressive in a touchy-feely sort of way; it tends to run on noble instincts rather than sound analysis. It cares about people, and it cares deeply about the harm that befalls them. Most importantly, the left does not trivialize the injury done by global capitalism. But it nevertheless fails to pivot politically from a sound take on capitalism *qua* capitalism. It is from these limited horizons that it enters debates, considers policy proposals and plans political strategies. To put this differently, it is not sensitive to the need to develop a foundational understanding of capitalism and its severe limitations, which can then frame and inform political discussions. The measure of politics for the left in Canada is often little more than a romanticized view of the Keynesian social policy framework of the 1960s. This is a Canada that is fondly recalled despite the fact that it is a Canada that never was, and a Canada that has long since passed by anyway.

A series of other grievous problems that beset the left have been thrown into relief in the neoliberal era. These problems are related to its failure to consider any alternatives to capitalism.

Eclipse of the Language of "Class"

It is difficult to establish a definitive link between the collapse of a negating political discourse in Canada and the concomitant eclipse of a class-based political discourse, but a number of factors have undoubtedly been at play. The fierce anti-communism of most of the twentieth century made it politically expedient to jettison the language of class, especially as notions like "working-class revolution" and "working-class emancipation through socialist revolution" were assailed in the mainstream cultural and political fora. To even talk about class issues or express sympathy with unions or the plight of workers was to risk inviting hostility and alienating potential voters conditioned by anti-communist hysteria. Even the non-communist left was regularly branded as "communist" and placed on a discredited political slope. This taboo has persisted for decades. To mention the "working class is forbidden from political talk," remarked American labour writer Steven Greenhouse, author of *The Big Squeeze: Tough Times for the American Worker*, in an interview on *Democracy Now* in the fall of 2008, "because people are going to be accused of being class warriors."[5] A pointed editorial in the *Monthly Review* applies as much to Canada as it does to the United States:

> Many on the left have indeed retreated from class and a vision of a democratic, egalitarian socialism. The important social issues of our day — race, gender and the environment — more often than not are divorced from the role of class structures. The rule of the capitalist class and the class struggle are shoved to the back burner. Whether consciously or not, the implicit assumption underlying the retreat from class is that capitalism will somehow or other go on and on as it creates miraculous new technology. Best then to stick to making those adjustments in social conditions that the system will presumably allow.[6]

This reluctance typifies the academy and has prompted some to use the language of "breaking cover" when speaking about issues in terms of class and class struggle.[7]

At the same time, "interest-aggregating parties," which embrace issues for the sake of garnering political support at the polls, have tended to emphasize cleavages and splits rather than commonalities among working people. NDPism, the watered-down version of social democracy in Canada, must also be counted in as a factor in the eclipse of a class-based political discourse. The highly corporatized media and the fawning professional milieu it encourages among journalists have certainly had their roles to play. And the economic changes within the working class itself, especially the relative decline of the traditional manufacturing job and the growth of the service sector and irregular employment, has helped to dull the class discourse in political life.

Reactionary Politics

The political agenda of the left today is largely reactionary, progressive to be sure, but reactionary nevertheless to the agenda of politics set by transnational capital. To each of the central elements of the neoliberal agenda the left has made its stand and defined its ambition: against unfettered free marketism it stresses the importance of maintaining some regulation and state control; against cut-backs it stresses the importance of restoring and retaining a full array of government services; against privatization it favours government expansion; against tax cuts it promotes adequately funded social programs; against corporate restructuring it draws attention to the social costs of de-industrialization, sub-contracting and short-term contracting; against rollbacks in labour laws it argues in favour of strengthening the regulatory regime; against elitism it favours expanded democratic reforms.

Decline of Left Parties

The radical left parties in Canada receive little support from the wider population, and the more popular social democratic alternative in Canada does not provide much traction for the development of a worker-friendly politics. The political orientation of the New Democratic Party offers little resistance to either neoliberalism or capitalism. It refuses to speak the language of class and class struggle, preferring instead the catch phrase "middle class" when speaking about the consequences of neoliberal policies. The NDP has even become a champion of some of the basic elements of the neoliberal agenda, for example, elevated concerns about government debt, which are used to ram home neoliberal reforms. A 2006 election post-mortem on the federal NDP by Dennis Pilon drew attention to the party and its anything-but-worker-friendly platform:

> Selling themselves as the "real" defenders of Canada's social programs, Layton's NDP promised to steer a "moderate" course on the economy, making some noises about corporate power but mostly amounting to a Blairite accommodation to the market and globalization. Gone were the allegedly controversial inheritance-tax proposals from the last campaign, as well as any real engagement with the economic problems facing "ordinary" Canadians.... The party arguably ran its most "mainstream" and neoliberal campaign ever: no tax increases, tough on crime, a mainstream economist running for the party and no mention of social democracy, let alone socialism.[8]

Not surprisingly, NDP governments elected at the provincial level have not stemmed the neoliberal onslaught.

Fragmentation

The wilting of the first wave of leftism in Canada included the aggressive marginalization of socialist and communist elements and the atrophy of social democracy. Well-meaning groups have stepped in to fight for the rights of migrant workers, female workers, low-wage workers, the poor, the working poor, welfare recipients and so forth. Other progressive organizations address such issues as environmental degradation. Local research and activist organizations like the Parkland Institute in Alberta have been complemented by nationally based organizations like the Canadian Centre for Policy Alternatives in an effort to draw attention to many of the issues facing oppressed groups, to attack the boasts of neoliberal apologists directly and to press for policy changes. Although these organizations generally oppose neoliberal policies, they also reveal the fragmentation and marginalization of the left. Without an enriching dialogue about capitalism in Canada, an informational network that counters the nonsense of the nightly news, a working-class culture that affirms the insights and experiences of working people and the coherent resistance of organized labour, *all* we are left with is a diverse collection of issue-based, resource-poor, small-scale organizations biting at the heels of the corporate Leviathan. They seem to accept that their concerns can be resolved at the policy level. They seem to accept that resistance against the abuses of capitalism is a cumulative process characterized by incremental successes, and they carry on despite their little headway year after year. To these groups the problems of capitalism are reduced to a series of "burning issues" urgently in need of attention. They work in relative isolation from one another, and there is little prospect that their efforts will galvanize into a movement capable of crossing a decisive political threshold. Through no fault of their own they are out of sight from a general public conditioned by the mass-mediated world of the CBC and CNN, and most of their efforts go unnoticed. They crave media attention — a mistake — and do not get much of it anyway. On the whole, they lack a political voice and press for changes with nothing more than moral authority at their disposal. They really are *all that's left* in Canada.

The Collapse of Labour

Those very institutions that throw the contradictory nature of capitalist society into relief have come to be little more than extensions of the productive process. Unions now merely shield individual workers from gratuitous abuse and summary discipline while faithfully delivering them to a productive sphere where the prerogatives of management and capital remain wholly intact. *Organized labour* has become an aspect of the *organization of labour* and little more, a wing of the exploitative process that smoothes out things. These historical expressions of working-class struggle have ossified into an arm of exploitative production. They effectively gift-wrap labour time in a manner that is appropriately pliant, docile and obedient. The radicalism and vision that attended much of the labour movement in the past, even if imperfectly, has been replaced by institutions that represent working people largely on the terms of their employers. Organized labour, as E.P. Thompson once wrote, is prone to feeding parasitically off the growth aspirations of the capitalist class, and in the neoliberal era this tendentiousness has been frequently confirmed.[9]

Combined with the redoubled aggression of neoliberalism against the working class, the capitulative political tendencies of organized labour have become the working class's greatest liability. Stories about sell-outs of the rank-and-file make the rounds. Workers occupy factories only to have the union leadership talk them down. Union leaders are trapped in legalistic straight-jackets partly of their own making. In the midst of this debacle all resistance seems to collapse. Solidarity is usually salutary: "I feel for your plight sister!" or "We wish you well in your strike brother!" As some union locals have been crushed their larger unions have proceeded in a business-as-usual manner. During the Irving Oil strike of the mid-1990s, Canada's equivalent of the Caterpillar strike in the U.S., the Communication, Energy and Paperworkers Union negotiated several other contracts with the Irving Group of Companies throughout the maritime provinces as the Saint John refinery workers were being pummelled. Protestations posted on websites have replaced sit-ins, marches, demonstrations and, most sadly, toughness during strikes. "Days of Action" and "Days of Disruption" are followed by weeks, months and even years of inaction. Sometimes the confusion on the part of organized labour boggles the mind, as when the Power Workers' Union came out in support of the Harris government during its dismantling of Ontario Hydro in the late 1990s. In the aftermath of the 2006 federal election, one commentator wrote without reserve about the political character of organized labour:

> This most recent election will go down in history as the one time the Canadian labour movement set a new record in ideological confusion. Buzz Hargrove hugged Paul Martin. A PSAC regional leader speculated on the benefits of electing Tories. Then, to top it all off, after the election the CLC issued a statement congratulating Harper and stating that all four parties, including the Conservatives, had 'addressed the concerns of working Canadians and working families,' especially on issues like women's equality, anti-scab legislation, pensions, health care, job creation, education and wages.[10]

At best, organized labour as a political force has withered. Such assessments even appear from those on the inside:

> Internally the union movement is not much of a movement these days, but a collection of individual unions pre-occupied with serving the members they have and competing with other unions for new members. As a movement, we are not in the lead when it comes to social issues or for fighting for the dignity and equality of all

workers.... We have been more engaged in fighting one another for membership than in finding ways to pull more workers into the union movement.[11]

A militantly organized labour movement could have challenged the neoliberal agenda. It utterly failed to have such a political presence. Only organized labour could have responded with something more than was done, by carrying an avowedly political message against capital and the political forces of neoliberalism directly into the "economy." Only strikes, sit-ins, sustained general strikes and marches backed by clearly articulated political messages could have stemmed the neoliberal tide. Nothing close to this ever happened.

Restoring and Deepening Left Culture

In many respects the restoration of *left culture* would mean the restoration of a pluralist left. It would move beyond today's truncated left, which has lost its political depth. Among other things the restoration of left culture would put the question of capitalism back on the table and enrich a politics of transformation. It could be said that culture must precede politics, that the restoration of left culture is a necessary condition for the restoration of left politics. Hence, the development of a rationally grounded left culture will precede a Gramscian-like counter-hegemonic struggle. There is little hope of cultivating a receptivity to transformative left policies until such a rationally grounded left culture congeals. To put this in more analytical terms, a vital left politics will emerge only after an intersubjective consciousness critical of capitalist social relations is forged. What I am suggesting is the promotion of a *left culturism* with an eye to the future, with the hope of encouraging what the esteemed sociologist John Porter dubbed a "creative politics" of class. The creation of a left culture is about the deepening of critical sensitivity in all matters of daily life. This revived culture will cradle a meaningful, proactive politics that confronts capitalism directly. My proposal is unlikely to help salvage much with respect to the present opportunity, which is passing us by. To minister to the policy demands of the present would be a mistake, a sacrifice of the possibility of more meaningful change in the future on the altar of opportunism, a sacrifice that will not achieve anything anyway. We have to see past this crisis of 2009 to better confront the post-neoliberal world down the road.

The following suggestions for restoring left culture include a rather surprising one about "quitting" politics altogether, a romantic one about striving to remember working-class history, a democratic one about giving voice to working people and two more commonplace suggestions about centring global citizenship and pushing for organized labour to exploit its latent capacity to disrupt things. There is nothing novel about these suggestions; the goal is to rebuild the left by restoring *left culture*. This culture would promote a discourse about the nature of capitalism, help to forge links between the different constituencies on the left, tap the vast potential of working people and celebrate the richness of our left heritage. Most significantly, this culture would help to tease out the radicalized consciousness of working people formed through their life experiences in a capitalist world.

Quit Politics

This peculiar suggestion for restoring the left has the following three elements:

The Left Requires a Rational Foundation

A healthy left politics *absolutely* requires open and reflective discussion, an intensive and exhaustive survey of history, an understanding of the left's past and its unique failures, an analysis of capitalism, an unrelenting commitment to education, a dialogue about the possibilities of change and the cultivation of strategies covering both the short and long terms. A rationally grounded left critique will promote the cultivation of "the suspecting attitude." It will encourage a healthy suspicion toward ideas and slogans generated in the context of the everyday culture industry. This politically sensitive culture will simultaneously de-construct the flood of mainstream messages and re-construct more worthy interpretations.

Most importantly, the "left" and "rational reflection" must go hand in hand for two reasons. First, working people may hold utterly contradictory sentiments about the world: "It is a rich man's world" and "unions are too powerful." These sentiments are in lockstep with the contradictions of capitalism. Recognizing that these contradictions of consciousness are lodged in everyone's head, a rational left culture must intervene assiduously to promote a resolution of the conflicting ideas. In the face of bloviating politicians and an equally windy right-wing media, far too many people conclude that job insecurity is the result of too much immigration or too much overseas production, or, in the face of homophobic diatribes, they become convinced that they should care deeply about the appropriate forms of sexual congress in God's eyes. A rationally formed left culture will do much more than merely counter such nonsense. A left culture rooted in an *ethos* of reflection will help to *resolve* these contradictory understandings and tease out truly critical sensibilities among all working people. Here the potential is vast. Despite the distortions of the mass mediated world, many people still arrive at the conclusion that politics itself looks like "mass distraction" and they still take a stand against war, union busting and so on. By this resilience we can be heartened. Indeed, it is only this resilience that has sustained the broken left in recent decades.

Second, capitalist society produces a litany of horrors and injustices that excite our emotions. Capitalism is troubling, and these emotions can carry us away. An *ethos* of reflection and contemplation will assuage the welter of emotions experienced by everyone, effectively absorbing our emotional distresses about capitalist life into a patient and reflective standpoint. A properly formed left culture is not unlike a properly formed Platonic soul, the soul where the faculty of reason governs the spiritedness and passion of our being. Passions are a part of life, but in capitalist society they can overtake us and must be massaged by reason, contemplation and sustained reflection.

In the Mass Mediated World Politics Is Entertainment

Conventional politics is inseparable from the world of entertainment and the culture industry. It is not so much that the terms of political discourse have shifted to the right in the last few decades, although this is certainly true. Rather, the terms of all political discourse have fallen from their loftier, more engaged and reflective heights of the past. The process was already well under way by the time the post-World War II order was established in North America, and largely coincides with the growth of the mass media. The rise of the television age in the 1950s intensified the problem.

Mass culture and entertainment are the natural allies of capitalist society insofar as they contribute to sustained consumption and promote the notion of the classless society, and political life has become part of this entertainment industry. Politics has been dumbed down to the level of meaningless protestations and empty slogans, to the "sound bite" and the puffed-up declaration, to the one-liner and the volley of vacuous phrases. Capitalism is the safer for this. At its best, the political media today is little more than a forum where the disciplining catchwords and stupefying mottos are rehearsed with varying degrees of anger, hostility or red-facedness. These lively but gentrified discussions merely stake out the field of acceptable discourse. In the world framed by CNN and the CBC the political pitfalls of a mass mediated life differ only by degree. In the media emotions are exploited while experiential dots are never connected; convictions are rehearsed but argumentative conclusions are never the goal; trip-wires of reaction are set but deliberation is never fostered; facts and events are adduced to reinforce "unshakable beliefs" and rarely brought forward to stimulate discussion. The citizen-viewer is meant to be either charmed or disgusted but never encouraged to develop a truly reflective and critical spirit.

The mainstream left has been drawn into this sphere of rational decay. The left is no less guilty of conducting politics at the level of name-calling, mythic misrepresentations of the past, imperialist and petty-nationalist euphemisms, comfortable turns of phrase, "magic words," shibboleths, sneering epithets and Orwellian "thought-stoppers." Completely lost in this irrational political world is a robust characterization of the character of global capitalist social relations, of the place of the Canadian social formation within it and of the required political responses to it.

The Left Must Quit Politics

Since leftism requires a rational, open discourse about the capitalist world and the nexus of the mainstream media and political discourse cannot facilitate this, there is no point in being a part of this system. When our political and cultural milieu can take Woody Guthrie's poetically anti-capitalist "This Land Is Your Land" and turn it into a children's song about the greatness of America, or parley Dylan's "The Times They Are a Changin'" into a ditty about the responsiveness of the banking industry to technological change, it clearly cannot sustain resistance against capitalism.

To revive itself the left must quit politics and quit thinking that the NDP or the Green Party offer anything that is politically redeemable. It must suspend its "civics" reflex and recognize that voting, circulating petitions and writing members of parliament are inconsistent with the cultivation of a meaningful left critique of capitalism in Canada. The natural seat of *left culturism* is the explanatory pamphlet, the week-end retreat, the study session, the free-school, the library and the church basement. Few lectures are worth attending unless you can take a sandwich and make a day of it. Blogospheres and "digital dissent" might help a bit, but not much. The internet should be used to network and post educational material. Rather than *Hockey Night in Canada*, we need "Left Afternoons in Canada," nation-wide socials sure to confound the mass media. Left television should resemble a community channel announcing lectures and other gatherings. This is how the left will begin afresh and renew itself from below. And we will know that a properly formed left culture is taking shape in Canada when the mass media and its news services cannot find the words to describe it.

This process will not be spectacular. The rehabilitation of the left in Canada must occur off the mainstream political grid — this is the only chance. In time there will be a fuller, rationally grounded political discourse that contributes to the growth and expansion of authentic working-class movements. Politics will again take on the richness that it once hinted at, and maybe, just maybe, political parties that are truly on the side of the working class will take shape, older parties will be revived and the act of voting will not be such a dispiriting waste of effort.

Strive to Remember

To revive itself the left must discover the working-class past. The ancient Greek historian Herodotus, sometimes called the "father of history," believed that societies naturally suffer from a deficit of memory. Thus he was motivated to record the deeds of men who valiantly defended the Greek world from the Persian invasions before they faded from living memory. More than 2,300 years later the celebrated German essayist Friedrich Nietzsche argued that Europe suffered from a surfeit of memory and that this excess had weakened the character of its people and repressed their "life-affirming instincts." Concern about social memory today is directed to the *politics of memory*. Social memory is never innocent but always tinged with a political purpose. Memory constitutes an increasingly significant part of the cultural consciousness that frames social practices and imbues those practices with meaning. The manner in which we narrate the *past* is very much a part of the *present* political struggle.

And yet, when we reflect on our inability to remember matters relating directly to working people we cannot help but think that Herodotus may have been on to something. We suffer from a deficit of memory when it come to working people and their achievements. We do rather well when it comes to erecting monuments to capitalist barons and their political supporters. But we forget about Winnipeg and the wave of strikes after World War I, the 1935 Trek to Ottawa and the One Big Union, just as we forget about Oshawa of 1937, Joe Beefs of Montreal, the Provincial Workmen's Association, the Glace Bay strike of 1925, the Workers' Unity League and figures like Paddy Draper, Joe Zuken and Maurice Spector. Forgetfulness about working-class achievements seems to be a sort of default setting for capitalist society.

The capitalist state does its part to insure that forgetfulness, as when it declared a sham day for working people, September's Labour Day, to replace May Day, a real worker's day, which passes by largely unobserved each year. When it so desires the state can pour vast resources into the orchestration of social memory. Each November 11, for example, sees a formal remembrance that rehearses the prevailing patriarchal narratives about the courage of soldiers and the importance of the sacrifices they have made to "safeguard freedom and democracy." The hallowed day is consecrated with all manner of solemnity and pageantry, and the ubiquitous poppy is impossible to miss during the first week of November. Officials declare that this day is really about preserving peace; "Lest we forget" is the expression that cautions the public about the importance of "remembering" so as to avoid future war. In fact soldiers' deeds are honoured in a highly cleansed way, and this day is really about preparing the next generation for war. We do not hear about the personal trauma and the deep psychological scarring soldiers experience, the severe strains soldiery places upon families and the financial hardships created by battlefield trauma, just as we fail to hear about the litany of battlefield depravities, such as rape, reprisal executions and extortion, that unfold in all war zones. Remembrance Day is a selective and politically motivated act of social recollection, and even to question the sanctity of this sacred day is to risk condemnation.

The Canadian state orchestrates this social remembrance, with its unifying motifs of *courage* and *sacrifice*. But there is no comparable effort to remember the *courage* and *sacrifice* of working people in Canada. We do not hear this language being used in the context of workers who courageously risked their lives and their livelihood by trying to form a union, of those who endured profound workplace abuse to feed their families, and especially of the many women who stood up to sexual predation in the workplace. We also fail to remember those workers who endured police abuse on the picket lines or sacrificed their lives in the "line of work." The notions of *courage* and *sacrifice*, along with many other inspiring qualities, could easily apply to the working-class past in Canada. To even suggest that we forget about the soldiers and remember the achievements of working people, however, is akin to committing treason.

Sheldon Currie's novella *The Glace Bay Miners' Museum* is set against the backdrop of the silence about the victimization of workers. It tells the story of a distraught woman who, in the aftermath of a mining accident that took the lives of her husband and brother, seeks to preserve the truth about abuse and class struggle by preserving representative body parts in jars of formaldehyde (her grandfather's blackened lungs, for example, since a doctor had once declared that he was fit to work). The woman, eerily, is hauled away by authorities at the end of the novel. The silences about the working-class past must be broken. Efforts have been afoot for several decades in the academy to recover this aspect of Canadian history. These discoveries need to become a part of everyday culture.

Celebrate the Winter Worker

A most striking thing unfolded during the Vietnam War years in the United States. In January 1971 American veterans started to gather in Detroit to tell their stories. Their accounts of the war become known as the Winter Soldier. They interrupted the prevailing narrative about the war and drew attention to the atrocities and war crimes that were being committed in Vietnam. This process was erected again during the more recent Gulf War in Iraq. The soldiers tell simple and plain truths about war — its horrors, confusions, depravities, injuries and mental scars. Their narrations are acts of peace.

Such storytelling is an indispensable part of the restoration of left culture, and it is equally crucial that it develops in the sphere of working life. Working people desperately need to tell their stories. Accounts of the experiences of workers in their own voice are relatively uncommon. Elliot Leyton's *Dying Hard: The Ravages of Industrial Society*, which outlines the suffering of mine workers in Newfoundland in the words of the miners themselves, is a rare example.[12] A renewed left must create venues that give working people a voice. This process will legitimate the experiences working people, who are generally ignored, draw attention to the quality of jobs, to counter the more typical quantitative emphasis on jobs, and explore the experiences of working people in detail, particularly the anxieties and fears that beset so many workers.

Become Citizens of the World

The history of capitalism and the history of nation-state sovereignty have been closely intertwined. What is striking about capitalism, however, has been its inexorable march to every region of the globe and its capacity to draw non-capitalist societies into the capitalist orbit. Although the term "globalization" has become fashionable in recent years, capitalism has been pushing out globally since its consolidation centuries ago. The search for new resources, the search for new markets, the exploitation of new pools of labour, the growth of local capitalist classes and the appearance of comprador bourgeoisies, and the patent domination of many regions in the South by the imperialist centres in the North have all contributed to the spread of capitalism around the world. In the first phases of this process Indigenous Peoples suffered horribly, as was certainly the case in the western hemisphere and Canada. As capitalism passes through its later phases of consolidation — roughly the middle of the nineteenth century in the Canadian case — a working class invariably arises. Although this process is still ongoing in some places, over time a global working class has arisen. This class is marked by the fact that their existence is entirely contingent upon their ability to sell their labour. In recent decades, with the ascendancy of transnational capital and its penchant for intra-firm trade and productive restructuring, the press of globalization and the concomitant consolidation of a global working class have intensified. Of course, "globalization" is the nice, safe, almost romanticized term that is used to describe this most recent process of capitalist expansion. Any analytical discussion that centres the domination of local capitalist classes in the North and the grotesque immiseration of working classes in the South, and that also emphasizes the typically brutal domination of the world's working people through military networks coordinated in the North, especially in the U.S., will be more inclined to use the term "imperialism."

In the imperialist age the horizons of capital are global. *As capital is internationalist in nature, so too must be left political struggles against it.* On this point, the left in Canada, by which is meant the left that must deploy its energies to confront capitalism in the social formation called Canada, faces its greatest hurdle. Most of what has ever called itself the left in Canada has been wrapped up in the flag. To some this nationalism has been its glaring albatross. If empathy is the rebel passion that drives the left in its grandest sense, then pride in one's country has been the taming instinct that creates political lassitude.

Perhaps if a truer image of Canada was portrayed this cleansing would be a little easier. Canada is merely a typical capitalist country with a typical history of oppression — despite its carefully crafted image as humanity's "poster country" for the forces of good. It is not unique and certainly not especially bad or especially good. These pedestrian political truths are concealed by the myths of the prevailing culture, including those about Canada's "peacefulness," particularly along the path of nation building. Much scholarship narrates the past as though the history of Canada has largely been about the forging of the nation. Even much critical scholarship seems to come to the conclusion that history has all been about securing the country and that, despite some rough spots here and there, there is still something in the Canada-that-has-come-to-be about which we can all be proud.[13] The left in Canada, moreover, has tended to gaze southwards rather than upwards, expressing concern about U.S. domination with much élan and intimating that a merry band of home-grown, robber barons would somehow make the country even better.

A rationally formed left will come to understand the political implications of the fact that the "achievement of nation" was not much on the mind of a woman "roughing it in the bush," an apprentice in the nineteenth century, an Irish immigrant helping to construct the Welland canal, a *patriote*, an organizer of unskilled workers in the early twentieth century, a victim of the residential schools system or a post-war European immigrant working in the construction sector, any more than it is likely to be much on the mind of a "temp" worker living in Vancouver, a struggling lone mother in Halifax, an unemployed auto-worker in Oshawa, a bureaucrat in Ottawa, a migrant worker from Mexico picking tomatoes in Leamington or a service worker struggling to pay rent in Calgary.

A rationally grounded left culture will help transfer the "fondness" for country to more worthy recipients, particularly working people and those who struggle against oppression in all of its guises in Canada and elsewhere. It will re-learn that the only appropriate starting point for analysis concerns the dynamics of imperialism and the necessity of a coordinated confrontation that extends beyond national boundaries, notwithstanding the fact that state policies continue to demand due attention. It will learn that the U.S. warrants special attention only because it is the centre of global imperialism and that Canada has played a considerable role in the construction of the global imperialist system. It will learn that corporations based in Canada have done their fair share of destruction and damage around the world. It will deepen its understanding of the similarities between exploited seamstresses in the Mexico and exploited janitors in Canada. It will come to appreciate that the expression of *solidarity* with struggling Indonesian workers loses its credibility when tied to an *oath of loyalty* to country and Queen. In any renewed left *solidarity must be worldly and seamless.*

Revive Organized Labour

In an interview with Maude Barlow marking the twentieth anniversary of the Council of Canadians, the dreadful failure of the left in the last three decades was indirectly disclosed. In commenting on the achievements of the Council, Barlow had this to say:

> We've had some tremendous wins. We stopped a big pension grab, we stopped the bovine growth hormone and we stopped the bank mergers. I can point to being deeply part of both Seattle and Cancun, where twice we stopped the World Trade Organization. I look at wins like stopping genetically engineered wheat and the Multilateral Agreement on Investment. I think that we've helped keep health care in public hands. These are big powerful wins that we accomplished with others.[14]

Immediately after this enumeration Barlow candidly added: "We've certainly lost a lot — *we haven't stopped the neoliberal agenda.*" This sobering admission is striking and desperately needs to be placed in a properly analytical context. For those a little further to the left there are many criticisms to be made of the Council of Canadians, including its reactionary agenda, its tiresome nationalism, its civics notion of political activism in "democratic" societies and its indefatigable faith in the redeemable nature of capitalism. But these limitations, which justify the criticism that it is ideologically eclectic at best, do not explain the failure of the Council or the left *in toto* to parry neoliberalism.

To account for this failure, we must ask why the avowedly nationalist and political Council of Canadians appeared at all in Canada? Why has the Council been forced to fight the neoliberal agenda? The answer to these questions draws attention to the political atrophy of the left in two crucial respects. First, we have seen the decay of a broad cultural left with spirited parties that combine to set the terms of political discourse. This failure, discussed extensively above, has created a political vacuum. The neoliberal era has witnessed intensive class struggle — capital squaring off against working people to ram home neoliberal policies — but no clearly marked "class politics." The political lacunae have been devastating for working people. The Council partially fills this void.

Second, organized labour failed to resist the agenda of the corporate world with the one strategy that could have stopped the neoliberal onslaught: strikes. Organized labour chose the path of *civil obedience* — and working people have paid dearly. One scholar has even linked the decline in union density in Canada to the declining militancy of the union movement and its loss of a political centre: "Union membership has declined in the last quarter-century chiefly because unions have increasingly fallen into the pockets of capital, have responded to structural shifts and employer/government assaults by acting more like managers and owners than like militant and upset workers, and thus have failed to come close to serving the inherently oppositional needs of their members."[15] An article on the CAW by Freda Coodin in *Canadian Dimension*, written before Buzz Hargrove negotiated the shocking "framework of fairness" with Magna International, captured many of the problems associated with organized labour today with impressive pith: "In spite of the occasional strong statement, the overriding message seems to be that there is no space for fighting anymore; no real point in reaching beyond defensiveness; no point in blaming the companies or making demands on them; no point in using the high-profile pulpit of negotiations to raise larger political demands around which the larger movement might be mobilized."[16] Again, the Council partially fills this void.

Absent robust working-class parties and a militant labour movement, an organization akin to the Council of Canadians was bound to have appeared. Resistance was left in the hands of an organization that could only engage in the occasional protest, issue press releases and publish literature on the harms of the neoliberal agenda. If organized labour had anything more than a rhetorical political presence on the Canadian political scene when the doyen of progressive luminaries established the Council of Canadians in the mid-1980s, it might never have formed, or at the very least it would have been considerably different The failure of the left owes much more to the politically dismal performance of organized labour than to the well-intentioned efforts of the Council of Canadians.

And so the challenge before us is paradoxical. A revitalized left would likely draw organized labour into a more militant posture, but that left is unlikely to be revitalized without organized labour being outwardly militant and aggressive. It is a difficult situation: greater militancy on the part of organized labour is necessary to stimulate and revitalize the left; a more coherent and revitalized left is more or less necessary to render organized labour more confident and aggressive. At the moment, sadly, we have neither. How can we loosen our Gordian knot? While organized labour is uniquely capable of bringing sustained pressure to bear on the agenda of capital, it is rendered inefficacious by conservative stewardship, a stewardship seemingly prone to an *iron law of buttoned-down caution*. This problem, in some ways, is endemic to all capitalist societies with liberal political veneers, that is, to societies where fear, vulnerability and anxiety unfold within institutions constrained by procedural and legal formalism. Changing this tendency on the part of organized labour is next to impossible. In its paroxysms the rank and file sometimes punches through the encrusted leadership to prevail, and sometimes labour leaders themselves summon the courage to run with the rank and file. But we cannot count on such irregularities to ever amount to much.

As for the other side of the paradox, however, there may be hope. Through the revitalization of a left culture the paradox can be softened, especially as a vibrant left culture promotes worker-friendly political organizations and parties. This twenty-first-century left will blend the best of the "old left" and the "new left." As the strategies suggested above encourage the development of a stable and enriched critique on the left, teasing out along the way the profound insight of working people into the nature of capitalist societies, the staid leadership of labour will be drawn along willy-nilly into a more militant posture. And then the energy of the left movement evident in social fora, issue-based organizations, political parties, some academics, activists and so forth will, at one and the same time, complement and reinforce an increasingly militant organized labour. The overall resistance to the agenda of capital will gather strength and deepen. The blossoming of this political movement will reflect the transformation of resignation and capitulation into reasonable optimism and meaningful solidarity. Salutations and website declarations will give way to real resistance. Only then will the face of the post-neoliberal world be stamped with a class politics that has finally caught up to the class warfare that has been waged for decades. And only then will the well-rehearsed ideals about Canada, ideals that presently warm the cockles of many a nationalist's heart, be exposed for what they really have always been — comfort myths contemptuous of both First Nations peoples and the working class. Most importantly, only then will the stage be set for further evolution of all things in the direction of a post-capitalist world. No one knows when this will happen, and the twilight of capitalism does not appear to be upon us at the moment, but things sometimes happen faster than we expect. We would do well to bear in mind that a rather sharp politico like Vladimir Lenin bemoaned the fact that he and his comrades would never see change in their lifetime, and commiserated so just a few weeks before the winter phase of the 1917 revolution began to unfold in Russia. Decades ago the conservative social thinker Eric Voegelin condemned socialism for "interiorizing the Christian eschatology," that is, for believing that a heaven-like world could be produced here on earth. To the Voegelins of the world we say: "Guilty as charged!" We can always count on capitalism to serve up depravity, cruelty and crisis, just as surely as we can count on it to engender responsive souls convinced that something much better awaits humanity on this planet. To the sensitive among us who have succumbed to this more immanent faith our struggle continues.

Notes

1. Richard Rorty, *Achieving Our Country: Leftist Thought in the 20th Century* (Harvard University Press, 1999), chapter 1 *in passim*. In keeping with his embrace of the American "pragmatic" tradition Rorty was very careful to stress that the only measure

of the left will be found in the effectiveness of its accomplishments. Left goals are true if they make the world a better place.

2. And this pleases the left. How assuaged would we be with reports of a law that forbade masters from whipping their slaves while leaving the system of slavery untouched?

3. Many examples of organizations characteristic of the second society are surveyed in Jack Quarter's *Canada's Social Economy: Co-operatives, Non-Profits and Other Community Enterprises* (Toronto: James Lorimer, 1992). However, not all of the organizations reviewed in Quarter's study reject the essential principles of capitalism, and many of them, like universities or professional business associations or organizations commonly identified as part of the "third sector," feed parasitically off the first society while contributing openly to its overall reproduction.

4. One of the best essays on this development is found in Michael S. Cross's introduction to *The Decline and Fall of a Good Idea: CCF-NDP Manifestoes 1932 to 1969* (Toronto: New Hogtown Press, 1974).

5. Steven Greenhouse, *The Big Squeeze: Steven Greenhouse on Tough Times for the American Worker*, Radio interview, *Democracy Now*, interviewed by Amy Goodman (New York: Pacifica Radio Network), July 29, 2008.

6. Editors, "Socialism: A Time to Retreat?" *Monthly Review* 52: 4 (September 2000), p. 1.

7. See the extended discussion in London Edinburgh Weekend Return Group, *In and Against the State* (London: Pluto Press, 1980), chapter 2.

8. See Dennis Pilon's commentary in "Election 2006: The NDP's Strategic Dead End," *Canadian Dimension* 40: 2 (March/April, 2006), quote from pp. 16–17.

9. E.P. Thompson, "Revolution," in *Out of Apathy*, E.P. Thompson, ed. (London, Stevens & Sons, 1960).

10. See Geoff Bickerton's discussion in "Labour and the Election," *Canadian Dimension* 40: 2 (March/April, 2006), quote from p. 10.

11. See the discussion in David Kidd, "State of the Unions 2005," *Canadian Dimension* 39: 3 (May/June 2005), quote from page 30.

12. Elliott Leyton *Dying Hard: The Ravages of Industrial Society* (Toronto: McClelland & Stewart Ltd., 1975).

13. For an example of this tendency, see Alvin Finkel and Margaret Conrad's *History of the Canadian Peoples: 1867–Present*, Volume II, (Toronto, Ontario: Pearson Education Canada Inc., 2002), where they write in the preface: "The third edition of *History of the Canadian Peoples* tries to preserve our primary object of an inclusive history of Canada. In addition to the achievements of the rich and powerful, we include developments in the lives of Aboriginal peoples, women, racial and ethnic minorities, and the poor, who also helped *to create the Canada we know today.*" p. xv, my emphasis. Notice also that no mention of "class" is made in this list.

14. Editorial Feature: Pathbreakers, "The Council of Canadians at 20," *Canadian Dimension* 39: 1 (January/February 2005), quotes from pp. 20–21.

15. Wythe Holt, "Union Densities, Business Unionism, and Working-Class Struggle: Labour Movement Decline in the United States and Japan, 1930–2000," *Labour* 59 (Spring 2007), p. 103.

16. See an excellent discussion in Freda Coodin, "The CAW Turn: Bargaining Versus Building," *Canadian Dimension* 39: 6 (November/December 2005), quote from p. 37.

Selected Bibliography

Abella, Irving (ed.). 1975. *On Strike: Six Key Labour Struggles in Canada 1919–1949*. Toronto: James Lorimer.

Aglietta, Michel. 1987. *A Theory of Capitalist Regulation*. London: Verso.

Barndt, Deborah. 2007. *Tangled Routes: Women, Work and Globalization on the Tomato Trail*. Rowman and Littlefield.

Bartlett, Eleanor. 1981. "Real Wages and the Standard of Living in Vancouver, 1901–1929." *B.C. Studies* 51 (Autumn): 3–62.

Bercuson, David Jay. 1990. *Confrontation at Winnipeg: Labour, Industrial Relations, and the General Strike*. McGill-Queen's University Press.

Bickerton, Geoff. 2006. "Labour and the Election." *Canadian Dimension* 40, 2 (March/April): 10.

Bienefeld, Manfred. 1994. "Capitalism and the Nation State in the Dog Days of the Twentieth Century." *Socialist Register*. London: The Merlin Press: 94–129.

Blackburn, Robin. 2008. "The Subprime Crisis." *New Left Review* 50 (March/April): 63–106.

Bliss, Michael. 1974. *A Living Profit: Studies in the Social History of Canadian Business, 1883–1911*. Toronto: McClelland and Stewart.

Bowles, Samuel. 1986. "Power and Profits: The Social Structure of Accumulation and the Profitability of the Postwar U.S. Economy," *Review of Radical Political Economics*, 18, 1-2:132-167.

Briskin, Linda. 2005. "The Work Stoppages Data from Human Resources and Skills Development Canada." *Just Labour* 5 (Winter): 80–89.

British Columbia Federation of Labour. 2001. *Employment Standards Review Discussion Paper*. December.

Brooks, Carellin. 1998. *Bad Jobs: My Last Shift at Albert Wong's Pagoda and other Ugly Tales of the Workplace*. Vancouver: Arsenal Pulp Press.

Brym, Robert J. 2003. "Affluence, Power, and Strikes in Canada, 1973–2000." In James Curtis, Edward Grabb and Neil Guppy (eds.), *Social Inequality in Canada: Patterns, Problems, Policies*. Fourth edition. Scarborough, Ontario: Prentice-Hall Canada.

Canadian Dimension editorial board. 2005. "The Council of Canadians at 20." *Canadian Dimension* 39, 1 (January/February): 20–25.

Cameron, Silver Donald. 1977. *The Education of Everett Richardson: The Nova Scotia Fishermen's Strike 1970–71*. Toronto: McClelland and Stewart Limited.

Campbell, Bruce. 2007. *20 Years Later: Has Free Trade Delivered on its Promise?* Ottawa: Canadian Centre for Policy Alternatives, North American Deep Integration Series, 1, 2 (December).

Card, David, and Alan Krueger. 1994. "Minimum Wages and Employment: A Case Study of the Fast Food Industry in New Jersey and Pennsylvania." *American Economic Review* 84, (September): 772–93.

Carrol, William K. 2007. "From Canadian Corporate Elite to Transnational Capitalist Class: Transitions in the Organization of Corporate Power." *The Canadian Review of Sociology and Anthropology* 44, 3 (August): 265–88.

Chang, Grace. 2000. *Disposable Domestics: Immigrant Workers in the Global Economy.* Boston: South End Press.

Coodin, Freda. 2005. "The CAW Turn: Bargaining Versus Building." *Canadian Dimension* 39, 6 (November/December): 36–38.

Copp, Terry. 1974. *The Anatomy of Poverty: The Condition of the Working Class in Montreal, 1897–1929.* Toronto: McClelland and Stewart.

Cross, Michael S. 1974. "Introduction." *The Decline and Fall of a Good Idea: CCF-NDP Manifestoes 1932 to 1969.* Toronto: New Hogtown Press.

De Kadt, Maarten. 2004. "The Paltry Wage in an Unfair System." *Review of Radical Political Economics* 36, 3 (Summer): 400–402.

Duménil, Gérard, and Dominique Lévy. 2002. "The Profit Rate: Where and How Much did it Fall? Did it Recover? (USA 1948–2000)." *Review of Radical Political Economics* 34: 437–61.

_____. 2004. "The Economics of US Imperialism at the Turn of the 21st Century." *Review of International Political Economy* 11, 4 (October): 657–76.

_____. 2004. "Neoliberal Income Trends: Wealth, Class and Ownership in the USA." *New Left Review* 30 (November/December): 105–33.

Fairey, David. 2005. *Eroding Worker Protections: British Columbia's New "Flexible" Employment Standards.* British Columbia: Canadian Centre for Policy Alternatives, November.

Fang, Tony, and Anil Verma. 2002. "Union Wage Premium." *Perspectives on Labour and Income* 14, 4 (Winter): 13–19.

Finkle, Alvin, and Margaret Conrad. 2002. *History of the Canadian Peoples: 1867–Present.* Volume 2. Toronto: Pearson Education Canada Inc.

Fudge, Judy. 2001. "Flexibility and Feminization: The New Ontario Employment Standards Act." *Journal of Law and Social Policy* 16: 1–22.

_____. 2003. "Labour Protection for Self-employed Workers." *Just Labour* 3 (Fall): 36–45.

Goldberg, Michael, and David Green. 1999. "Raising the Floor: The Social and Economic Benefits of Minimum Wages in Canada." British Columbia: Canadian Centre for Policy Alternatives. September.

Gordon, David. 1980. "Stages of Accumulation and Long Economic Cycles." In Terence K. Hopkins and Immanuel Wallerstein, eds., *Processes of the World System.* Beverly Hills: Sage Publications.

Gray, Anne. 1998. "New Labour — New Labour Discipline." *Capital and Class* 65 (Summer): 1–8.

Greenberg, Jerald. 1990. "Employee Theft as a Reaction to Underpayment Inequity: The Hidden Cost of Pay Cuts." *Journal of Applied Psychology* 75, 5: 561–68.

Greer, Alan. 1985. "Wage Labour and the Transition to Capitalism: A Critique of Pentland." *Labour/Le Travail* 15 (Spring): 7–22.

Guard, Julie. 2008. "How Important Are Labour-Friendly Laws to Manitoba's Unions?" *Labour Notes.* Winnipeg: Canadian Centre for Policy Alternatives, July.

Harrod, Jeffrey. 1987. *Power, Production and the Unprotected Worker.* New York: Columbia University Press.

Heron, Craig. 1996. *The Canadian Labour Movement: A Short History.* Second edition. Toronto: James Lorimer.

Hibbs, Douglas A. 1978. "On the Political Economy of Long-Run Trends in Strike

Activity." *British Journal of Political Science* 8, 2 (April): 153–75.

High, Steven. 2003. *Industrial Sunset: The Making of North America's Rust Belt, 1969–1984.* Toronto: University of Toronto Press.

Holt, Wythe. 2007. "Union Densities, Business Unionism, and Working-Class Struggle: Labour Movement Decline in the United States and Japan, 1930–2000." *Labour* 59 (Spring): 99–131.

Jamieson, Stuart. 1968. *Times of Trouble: Labour Unrest and Industrial Conflict in Canada, 1900–1966.* Ottawa, Task Force on Labour Relations.

Kidd, David. 2995. "State of the Unions 2005." *Canadian Dimension* 39, 3 (May/June): 29–32.

Klein, Seth, and Barbara Montgomery. 2001. *Depressing Wages: Why Welfare Cuts Hurt Both the Welfare and the Working Poor.* British Columbia: Canadian Centre for Policy Alternatives. March.

Knight, David, and Darren McCabe. 2000. "Ain't Misbehavin'? Opportunities for Resistance Under New Forms of 'Quality' Management." *Sociology* 34, 3: 421–36.

Kotz, David M. 1994. "The Regulation Theory and the Social Structure of Accumulation Approach." In David M. Kotz, Terrence McDonough and Michael Reich (eds.), *Social Structures of Accumulation: The Political Economy of Growth and Crisis.* Cambridge University Press.

Kotz, David M., and Martin H. Wolfson. 2004. "Déjà Vu All Over Again: The 'New' Economy in Historical Perspective." *Labor Studies Journal* 28, 4 (Winter): 25–44.

Langille, David. 1987. "The Business Council on National Issues and the Canadian State." *Studies in Political Economy* 24 (Autumn).

Laxer, James. 1999. *The Undeclared War: Class Conflict in the Age of Cyber Capitalism.* Toronto: Penguin Books.

Leyton, Elliott. 1975. *Dying Hard: The Ravages of Industrial Society.* Toronto: McClelland & Stewart.

Lipietz, Alain. 1987. *Mirages and Miracles: The Crises of Global Fordism.* Trans. David Macey. London: Verso.

Lippit, Victor D. 2004. "Class Struggles and the Reinvention of American Capitalism in the Second Half of the Twentieth Century." *Review of Radical Political Economics* 36, 3 (Summer): 336–43.

Little, Margaret. 1998. *No Car, No Radio, No Liquor Permit: The Moral Regulation of Single Mothers in Ontario, 1920–1997.* Toronto: Oxford University Press.

London Edinburgh Weekend Return Group. 1980. *In and Against the State.* London: Pluto Press.

Luke, Helesia, and Graeme Moore. 2004. *Who's Looking Out for Our Kids?: Deregulating Child Labour Law in British Columbia.* British Columbia: Canadian Centre for Policy Alternatives. March.

MacDowell, Laurel Sefton, and Ian Radforth. 2000. *Canadian Working Class History: Selected Readings.* Second edition. Toronto: Canadian Scholars Press.

McCallum, E. 1986. "Keeping Women in Their Place: The Minimum Wage in Canada, 1910–1925." *Labour/Le Travail* 17 (Spring): 29–56.

McDonough, Terrence. 2008. "Social Structures of Accumulation Theory: The State of the Art." *Review of Radical Political Economics* 40, 2 (Spring): 153–73.

McIntyre, Richard, and Michael Hillard. 2008. "The 'Limited Capital-Labour Accord': May it Rest in Peace." *Review of Radical Political Economics* 40, 3 (Summer): 244–49.

Mizen, Phil. 1994. "In and Against the Training State." *Capital and Class* 53 (Summer): 99–121.

Monthly Review. 2000. "Socialism: A Time to Retreat?" *Monthly Review* 52: 4 (September): 1–7.

Moody, Kim. 1997. *Workers in a Lean World: Unions in the International Economy.* New York: Verso.

Moseley, Fred. 1999. "The United States Economy at the Turn of the Century: Entering a New Era of Prosperity." *Capital and Class* 67 (Spring): 25–45.

Moulton, David. 1975. "Ford Windsor — 1945." In Irving Abella (ed.), *On Strike: Six Key Labour Struggles in Canada 1919–1949*. Toronto: James Lorimer.

Mulholland, Kate. 2004. "Workplace Resistance in an Irish Call Centre: Slammin', Scammin', Smokin' an' Leavin'." *Work, Employment and Society* 18, 4 (December): 709–24.

Myers, Gustavus. 1972. *A History of Canadian Wealth*. Volume 1. Toronto: J. Lewis & Samuel.

Navarro, Vincent. 2006. "The Worldwide Class Struggle." *Monthly Review* 58, 4 (September): 18–33.

Ogmundson, R., and M. Doyle. 2002. "The Rise and Decline of Canadian Labour, 1960 to 2000: Elites, Power, Ethnicity and Gender." *Canadian Journal of Sociology* 27, 3: 413–53.

Organization for Economic Cooperation and Development. 2008. *Growing Unequal? Income Distribution and Poverty in OECD Countries*. OECD, October.

Palmer, Bryan D. 1987. "Labour Protest and Organization in Nineteenth-Century Canada, 1820–1890." *Labour/Le Travail* 20 (Fall): 61–83.

_____. 1992. *Working Class Experience: Rethinking the History of Canadian Labour, 1800–1991*. Second edition. Toronto: McClelland and Stewart.

_____. 2003. "What's Law Got to do with it? Historical Considerations on Class Struggle, Boundaries of Constraint, and Capitalist Authority." *Osgoode Hall Law Journal* 41, 2 & 2: 465–90.

Panitch, Leo, and Donald Swartz. 2003. *From Consent to Coercion: The Assault on Trade Union Freedoms*. Third edition. Toronto: Garamond.

Pentland, H. Clare. 1959. "The Development of a Capitalistic Labour Market in Canada." *Canadian Journal of Economics and Political Science* 25: 450–61.

Perkins, John. 2006. *Confessions of an Economic Hit-Man*. New York: Plume.

Pierson, Ruth Roach. 1990. "Gender and the Unemployment Insurance Debates in Canada, 1930–1940." *Labour/Le Travail* 25 (Spring): 77–103.

Piketty, Thomas, and Emmanuel Saez. 2003. "Income Inequality in the United States, 1913–1998." *The Quarterly Journal of Economics* 118, 1 (February): 1–39.

Pilon, Dennis. 2006. "Election 2006: The NDP's Strategic Dead End." *Canadian Dimension* 40, 2 (March/April): 16–18.

Porter, Ann. 2003. *Gendered States: Women, Unemployment Insurance, and the Political Economy of the Welfare State in Canada, 1945–1997*. Toronto: University of Toronto Press.

Pulkingham, Jane. 1998. "Remaking the Social Divisions of Welfare: Gender, 'Dependency' and UI Reform." *Studies in Political Economy* 56 (Summer).

Quarter, Jack. 1992. *Canada's Social Economy: Co-operatives, Non-Profits and Other Community Enterprises*. Toronto: James Lorimer.

Rinehart, James W. 2006. *The Tyranny of Work: Alienation and the Labour Process*. Fifth edition. Toronto: Thomson Nelson.

Robinson, William I. 2004. *A Theory of Global Capitalism: Production, Class, and State in a Transnational World*. Baltimore: The Johns Hopkins University Press.

Rorty, Richard. 1999. *Achieving our Country: Leftist Thought in the 20th Century*. Cambridge,

MA: Harvard University Press.

Scott, Katherine. 1996. "The Dilemma of Liberal Citizenship: Women and Social Assistance Reform in the 1990s." *Studies in Political Economy* 50 (Summer): 7–36.

Shalla, Vivian (ed.). 2006. *Working in a Global Era: Canadian Perspectives.* Toronto: Canadian Scholar's Press.

Shalla, Vivian, and Wallace Clement (eds.). 2007. *Work in Tumultuous Times: Critical Perspectives*. Montreal, Kingston: McGill-Queen's University Press.

Shields, John. 1996. "Flexible Work, Labour Market Polarization, and the Politics of Skill Training and Enhancement." In Dunk et al. (ed.), *The Training Trap: Ideology, Training and the Labour Market.* Halifax: Fernwood Publishing.

Sklair, Leslie. 2001. *The Transnationalist Capitalist Class.* Malden, MA: Blackwell Publishers.

Slinn, Sara. 2003. "The Effect of Compulsory Certification Votes on Certification Applications in Ontario: An Empirical Analysis." *Canadian Labour and Employment Law Journal* 10, 3: 399–429.

Smart, Josephine. 1997. "Borrowed Men on Borrowed Time: Globalization, Labour Migration and Local Economies in Alberta." *Canadian Journal of Regional Science* (Spring/Summer): 141–60.

Smith, Douglas A. 1972. "The Determinants of Strike Activity in Canada." *Industrial Relations* 27, 4: 663–77.

Smith, Murray E. 2000. "Political Economy and the Canadian Working Class: Marxism or Nationalist Reformism?" *Labour/Le Travail* 46 (Fall): 343–68.

Swift, Jamie. 1995. *Wheel of Fortune: Work and Life in the Age of Falling Expectations.* Toronto: Between the Lines.

Tangri, Beverly. 1978. "Women and Unemployment." *Atlantis* 3, 2 (Spring).

Thomas, Henk (ed.). 1995. *Globalization and Third World Trade Unions: The Challenge of Rapid Economic Change.* New Jersey: Zed Books.

Thomas, Mark. 2004. "Setting the Minimum: Ontario's Employment Standards in the Postwar Years, 1944–1968." *Labour/Le Travail* 54 (Fall): 49–82.

Thompson, E.P. 1960. "Revolution." In E.P. Thompson (ed.), *Out of Apathy.* London: Stevens and Sons.

Vosko, Leah F. 1998. "Regulating Precariousness?: The Temporary Employment Relationship Under the NAFTA and the EC Treaty." *Relations industrielles* 53, 1: 123–53.

_____. (ed.). 2007. *Precarious Employment: Understanding Labour Market Insecurity in Canada.* McGill-Queen's University Press.

Warren, Jim. 2008. *Joining the Race to the Bottom: An Assessment of Bill 6, Amendments to the Trade Union Act, 2008.* Canadian Centre for Policy Alternatives, Saskatchewan Office. March.

Webber, M.J., and D.L. Rigby. 1986. "The Rate of Profit in Canadian Manufacturing, 1950–1981." *Review of Radical Political Economics* 18, 1 & 2: 33–55.

Wolfe, David. 1984. "The Rise and Demise of the Keynesian Era in Canada: Economic Policy, 1930–1982." In Michael S. Cross and Gregory S. Kealey (eds.), *Modern Canada, 1930–1980s.* Toronto: McClelland and Stewart.

Wolfson, Martin. 2003. "Neo-liberalism and the Social Structure of Accumulation." *Review of Radical Political Economics* 35, 3 (Summer): 255–62.

Index